THE EUROPEAN
RENAISSANCE
SINCE 1945

THE EUROPEAN
RENAISSANCE
SINCE 1945

MAURICE CROUZET

with 144 illustrations, 12 in color

HARCOURT BRACE JOVANOVICH, INC.

1 *Frontispiece*
One aspect of European revival:
modern housing in
Hansa Viertel, West Berlin

Translated from the French by Stanley Baron

Picture research: Georgina Bruckner

3-10-75

Library of Congress Catalog Card Number: 70–98534

ISBN 0–15–524780–8 Paperbound
ISBN 0–15–129360–0 Hardbound

Printed and bound in Great Britain by Jarrold & Sons Ltd, Norwich

CONTENTS

PREFACE 7

I THE CONDITION
OF EUROPE IN 1945 9

II SUCCESSES 16

III CHANGES IN SOCIETY 103

IV INTELLECTUAL
AND CULTURAL LIFE 135

V THE WEAKNESSES 167

VI BALANCE SHEET 195

BIBLIOGRAPHICAL NOTES 204

LIST OF ILLUSTRATIONS 209

INDEX 212

In the following pages the reader will find a survey of the revival of Europe since 1945. In only a few years, this devastated, decimated, famished continent achieved a prosperity it never knew before, its material and intellectual forces regained their strength, while the impact of industrial civilization, following the American model, imposed wide-ranging economic and social changes. How did such a recovery come about? The first part of this book tries to answer that question. The second indicates, on the contrary, that this brilliant picture may not be so definitive as appears at first sight: internal dangers and a world situation which threatens to deteriorate every day, make the achievement precarious, unless the states of Europe can form a union comparable to those of the USA and the USSR, which have shown that unity is the very condition of effectiveness.

The select bibliography at the end of the book mentions those to whom this study owes much; I wish to express my debt to them. Since the USSR has been dealt with in another volume in this series, J. P. Nettl's *The Soviet Achievement*, I have not thought it necessary to treat that country in any detail before the terminal date of his book, 1967.

MAURICE CROUZET
Paris, July 1970

◀ 2 *Destroyed City*, symbolic sculpture by O. Zadkine in Rotterdam, target of German saturation bombardment during the Second World War

I THE CONDITION OF EUROPE IN 1945

At the moment when military operations ceased in Europe, the continent offered a spectacle of desolation. Material destruction, the enormous displacement of population, the systematic massacre of millions of people, as well as moral and intellectual ruin, had brought about complete chaos. No one could have imagined that Europe would recover for a long time. Within the vast territory occupied by the Germans, from Brest to the gates of Leningrad and the borders of the Caucasus, from the North Cape to the Egyptian frontier, the material devastation resulting from military operations had accumulated. It was particularly severe in the USSR and Poland, in eastern Germany, Yugoslavia, the battle-zone of Normandy, the Netherlands, the Ardennes in Alsace, the left bank of the Rhine, and also in the combat areas of southern and central Italy. But deep traces had also been left by bombing raids undertaken to demoralize the civilian population (London, Rotterdam, Coventry, Dresden), to destroy war factories or to pave the way for Allied landings (railway stations, all ports except for Antwerp and Bordeaux, railway tracks, almost all bridges, road junctions, etc.); and by the struggles of resistance groups and partisans against troops on reprisal or repression operations. And there was no way of assessing the damage afflicted by the 'scorched-earth' policy on channels of communication, transport equipment, factories and mines, warehouses and crops.

Even this catalogue of destruction does not give a complete picture of Europe's wreckage; one must also take into account the factory equipment, dismantled and transported to Germany, which was ruined by overuse and the shortage of lubricants. Moreover, after the war the victors tried to retrieve either the actual equipment of which they had been despoiled, or its equivalent: whole factories were dismantled and emptied of their machinery, while locomotives, rolling stock, trucks and raw materials were taken over by the plundered countries.

Industry and transport were not the only activities reduced to a state of non-production: the soil itself had been deeply affected.

3, 4 War destruction. Above, ruins of Dresden after Allied air action; below, refugees from siege-stricken Leningrad

First of all, the battle-zones, sown with mines or other military installations, and often flooded, had remained uncultivated and were too dangerous to put back into cultivation immediately. The lack of fertilizers, plus the scarcity of farm labour and draught animals, had caused an alarming drop in yield and production (half the output for 1935–39) from over-exploited soil. German requisitions had decimated the cattle population, and inadequate feeding had reduced their yield of milk and beef.

Strategic bombing had destroyed or damaged millions of dwellings: 20 per cent in France and the Netherlands, 30 per cent in Great Britain, 40 per cent in Germany. The shortage of transport aggravated the difficulties of food supplies to both cities and specialized industrial or wine-growing regions. All that could be maintained were barter relations between city and country, so that famine was a threat everywhere.

To this scene of material destruction we can add the political chaos and the insecurity caused in many parts of Europe by the fall of dictatorial regimes that had opted for Nazism or Fascism. Administrations in most countries were disorganized, public finances in confusion, governments weakened or overthrown. A dismembered Germany was deprived of any central government, and local authorities were strictly subordinated to the victors who appointed them. The Balkan states were in a similar situation. Even when former governments remained, they undertook vigorous measures of denazification and began to follow the path of Communism. Poland was harrowed, Italy was largely administered by the American Occupation Forces and partially abandoned to the Mafia and brigands; in France reprisals against collaborators and the difficulty of liaison with the organs of central government sustained an atmosphere of passionate conflict and deep disorder, much greater than in the Netherlands, Norway and Denmark, whose governments had emigrated to Great Britain and preserved their authority. This was also true of Belgium, although there the dynastic problem gravely disturbed the political atmosphere. Great Britain alone, among the victorious and defeated European powers, experienced no political upheaval. As for the neutrals – Sweden, Switzerland, Ireland, Portugal – they, too, had no disturbances, but for quite different reasons. Spain, which had suffered heavy losses in human lives during the Civil War, remained overwhelmed with material destruction, and this made the prolonged and ruthless repression of all 'wrong-thinkers' still worse.

5 Partisan prisoners:
print by Renato Guttuso

6 *The Hanged Partisan*,
a bronze bas–relief by G. Manzù

7 Polish poster commemorating war–dead

Civilian populations had suffered appreciable losses, not only in the numbers of injured or killed, but also as a result of panics which hurled them on to the road without provisions or adequate transportation, placing them at the mercy of epidemics and the lack of food and shelter. To losses of this nature, which had been meagre during the First World War and are difficult to estimate accurately for the Second (except that we know they were much higher), we must add the loss of lives caused by the war itself and the Nazi policy of genocide: soldiers killed or left permanently disabled; deaths from wounds, disease or cold; political deportees, Jews, gipsies, Russian and Polish prisoners in particular, who were killed immediately or reduced to slow extinction in death-camps. In the district of Kaluga in the USSR, 35 per cent of the population had been deported, and in 1957 there were no more than 50 able-bodied men per *kolkhoz* as compared with a normal average in the Balkans of 293. All these factors appear to have deprived Europe of nearly 30,000,000 people, to which must be added the decline of population resulting from the reduced number of births.

These losses in human lives and productivity would be enough to explain the general scarcity caused by the desolation of the European economy and the poor state of health of the populations that survived. But the European economy, affected ever since 1929 by the great world depression and beginning only in 1939 to recover from a terrible crisis of unemployment and underproduction, was now plunged into even more serious chaos by two additional factors: (1) by the overthrowing of existing frontiers, which destroyed traditional economic relationships, separating suppliers and consumers, and (2) by the dismemberment of certain countries, such as Poland, Germany and Rumania, whose physiognomy was completely changed. The loss of overseas markets must also be taken into account. The countries of South and Central America, deprived of European manufactures during the war, turned instead to the United States and Canada, while they sold their raw materials and food products to the belligerents at greatly increased prices. African and Asian colonies, more or less cut off from their mother-countries, also turned towards the United States, which began to establish itself solidly in markets it had not penetrated before. Finally, the countries that produced precious raw materials took advantage of their gains to repay some of their debts and became creditor rather than debtor nations. Thus the European states were doubly impoverished – first, through the disappearance of a part of their foreign investments and revenues which had re-established the equilibrium of their yearly balance of payments, and second, through the loss of markets which they would never again be able to regain completely. Their prestige had also suffered greatly. The savage and swift defeat of the great powers that had dominated the world in 1939 dealt a mortal blow to their influence; the beneficiaries of this were Japan (in spite of the brutality of its rule in those countries it had temporarily conquered) and, above all, the USA and the USSR. The respect enjoyed by the European great powers, whose strength had been regarded as invincible, was destroyed in 1939 and 1940; henceforward the colonial peoples – even those which had remained loyal to the mother-country while the war was on – claimed their independence, encouraged by the Atlantic Charter and by the diplomatic or other agents of the two great victors, the USA and the USSR.

The most disastrous aspect of the post-war economy in Europe was the deterioration of the financial and monetary situation. This resulted from the enormous circulation of paper money and the credit inflation, which had been the accompaniment of war expenditures or, in the occupied countries, of pillage effected under cover of occupation indemnities and credit clearances. Up to the end of the war this inflation had not exercised any substantial influence on price levels, because strict control and rigorous penalties maintained the stability of prices or limited their rise. The inflationist potential nevertheless remained considerable. After the liberation, as soon as the system of price-control disappeared, a gulf opened between excess purchasing power and the extreme scarcity of products for sale, a disparity which gave a powerful stimulus to inflation.

Another formidable factor in the dislocation of the social and economic structure had its origin in the deportation of millions of foreign workers to German factories and the expulsion of the populations of annexed areas.

The moral and political devastation had heavy consequences in the occupied countries and in Germany after its defeat. It was seen in social and national dislocation; in the accentuation of class and regional antagonisms; in the rupture, principally in France, the Netherlands, Denmark and Norway, of the traditional democratic order, of the habit of liberty, respect for individual rights, and the independence of the judiciary. Although it may have been short-lived, the rule of a military or police dictatorship without curbs was contagious and had a demoralizing effect; it instilled, especially among the young, habits of violence and illegality which, in perpetuating themselves, increased the difficulties of reconstructing the economy as well as restoring political and social order.

As for eastern Europe, it had been subjected by the Nazis for many long years to a particularly savage exploitation; in general, the situation there was even worse than that in the western part of the continent. Considerable numbers of the inhabitants had been either deported or replaced by German colonists, or else exterminated, as in Poland. In the USSR, those whose loyalty was considered suspect had been removed to Asia. Finally, eastern Europe had been the battlefield of two enemy armies, neither of which had any interest in the welfare of the people or their resources. On the contrary, in the course of their retreats both armies had used 'scorched-earth' tactics.

Moreover, after the end of hostilities Europe was divided into two separate parts by the demarcation line established between the territories liberated or occupied respectively by the Western Allies

or the USSR. This separation continued after the customs unification of the western occupation zones (1948); with the advent of the Cold War, caused by the rivalry of the USA and the USSR, the two Europes of east and west were divided by the 'iron curtain'. Reconstruction and development in the two parts of Europe were consequently very different, because of the differences in political and economic doctrines, as well as in the social structure that naturally emerged from them.

Devastated and deeply divided, economically and politically out of balance, Europe in 1945 was threatened with social and political disturbances, not only because of poverty and want, but also because of bitterness against the privileged classes who had often supported the victor of the moment or had at least easily accommodated themselves to the defeat which, as they thought, protected them against the contagion of revolution. Europe in 1945 was a beggar supported by its American ally, incapable of revival through its own powers.

8 *Europe after the Rain II*, painting by Max Ernst (1940–42)

II SUCCESSES

This debilitated Europe, which, to all appearances, would be dependent for a long time, was nevertheless to experience a more rapid and complete material recovery than anyone would have dared to predict. And the stages of this recovery, which United Nations experts had forecast for the decade 1949–59, were achieved well in advance of that date. Moreover, after a few years Europe was to enjoy a prosperity far greater than any in its past.

Recovery took place progressively. Little by little, the social agitation following liberation subsided, and the hopes of resistance movements to create a more human and just structure were dissipated. The frequent strikes in France in 1947, and in Italy in 1950 and 1951, calmed down; the Socialist and Communist Parties, which were strong in certain countries, gave orders of moderation to their adherents ('You have to know how to end a strike,' said Maurice Thorez, leader of the French Communists), and these orders were followed. All parties were inspired by the feeling that the most urgent task was to restore means of communication and the circulation of goods, to reconstruct factories and to reconstitute their equipment and stocks of raw materials. The passionate hostility shown in some countries against employers and members of the executive class who had been considered too complaisant *vis-à-vis* the Nazis and the governments that collaborated with them, had a tendency to weaken. The Communist Parties in Italy and France, where they drew a certain prestige from the major role they had played in the struggle against the German *Wehrmacht*, joined in the post-war governments, thus facilitating pacification. In south-eastern Europe power passed into the hands of national Communist Parties that undertook economic reconstruction in accordance with Socialist principles.

Only one country, Greece, was prey to civil war. There the ELAS resistance movement clashed with the monarchists, who were given military support first by Great Britain, then by the United States.

9 *Liberation*, painting by Ben Shahn (1945)

10 Red Army tanks entering Theresienstadt in Czechoslovakia in the closing stages of the war

11 *Liberation, May 1945*, relief by the Danish sculptor Henrik Starcke

But when Marshal Tito's aid to ELAS came to an end, the revolutionaries had to cease fighting and were ruthlessly repressed. The social tension revived by the Cold War, which prevailed particularly in 1948 at the time of the Berlin blockade and the Communist *coup d'état* in Prague, and then again during the Korean War (1950–53), relaxed even before Stalin's death in 1953. The political détente became more marked in the following years. There were eruptions of tension of varying length and violence, but never serious enough to threaten the social peace that the governments (in general, conservative) of western Europe maintained with little difficulty in spite of monetary crises and the rising cost of living. As for the Communist countries, the organization of their economy on new principles was carried out in the face of difficulties and delays caused by the American blockade and the prohibition of the delivery of so-called 'strategic materials' by the allies of the United States. Nevertheless, this measure slowed down very considerably the rate at which the Communist countries of eastern Europe could re-equip themselves and obtain raw materials and food products.

RECONSTRUCTION

12 The centre of West Berlin: the stump of the old, and the tower of the new, Kaiser Wilhelm Memorial Church

13, 14 Polish and Hungarian posters expressing the post-war reconstruction effort

15 New buildings in a heavily bombed area of London

Another factor contributed significantly to the economic revival: this was, paradoxically, the decline of doctrinaire liberalism. Even while theoreticians and statesmen proclaimed their defence of free enterprise and denial of any state interference in the economy, they were nonetheless forced by necessity and the urgent need to take decisions to accept state intervention in the economic sphere. Manufacturers and merchants, however, were encouraged by the American government, which praised the benefits of free enterprise and multiplied its invitations to visit and verify its successes on the spot, thus offering to numerous missions of company managers and executives the spectacle of a prosperity unknown to Europe. This approval of economic liberalism was echoed among consumers who had long been rationed, deprived of imported products they had been used to, and were now encouraged by salary rises obtained immediately after the liberation and by the abundance of paper money. The return to ease took place too soon and could not last, for inflation grew and money depreciated. Each state had to adopt a plan of reconstruction priorities and establish an import scheme giving greatest urgency to raw materials and essential foodstuffs. Only the state was capable of taking this task in hand and of enforcing the preponderance of the general good over particular interests. Businessmen, most often reluctantly, had to accept this intervention – all the more since civil peace depended upon full employment, decent salaries, and the disappearance of arbitrary methods in personnel direction. Moreover, the working class, who feared more than anything the return of unemployment, had become strong enough to demand and enforce either confirmation of existing social legislation (e.g., in Germany and Great Britain) or full implementation of measures outlined in the late 1930s as a remedy for the great depression (in France, the Matignon agreements and collective contracts).

THE REPATRIATION OF POPULATIONS

Parallel with the restoration of the means of production, the great mass of displaced persons – possibly 30,000,000, according to Kulischer's calculations – began to be repatriated. These were people who had been driven from their homes and countries by the violence of the fighting, by invasion and the 'scorched-earth' policy, by political and social upheavals. Migrations on a scale never known before in Europe – even during the Middle Ages – had affected dozens of millions of human beings, in particularly inhuman conditions:

prisoners of war of all nationalities, survivors of deportation camps, forced labourers from all countries, Frenchmen expelled from Alsace-Lorraine, Soviet populations transferred to Siberia as a precautionary measure when the German armies were approaching, 'collaborators' in various countries who had run away from justice. Besides these repatriates there were Karelians, Finns, Lapps from Norway, Swedes in Estonia, who had fled before the Soviet advance; Germans scattered, in some cases since the Middle Ages, in Poland, Rumania and Hungary, plus all those who had been sent by Hitler to colonize Poland and the Ukraine; Rumanians transferred to Transnistria, Bukovina or Bessarabia. In the west there were Germans who had taken heel at the Allies' advance, repeating the pitiful spectacle of the Belgians and the French in 1940 – in summer, it is true – on the roads of France.

Then there were populations expelled as undesirable according to the Potsdam agreement. About 6,500,000 *Volksdeutsche* were driven out of eastern countries where they had constituted important national minorities; between the two wars, these people had shown a doubtful loyalty and, when the moment came, had betrayed their countries with German support. Poland, sharing borders with Lithuania, Bielorussia and the Ukraine, had ethnic minorities which formed over 30 per cent of the total population; in Czechoslovakia, Czechs and Slovaks represented only two-thirds of the population; in Rumania 5,000,000 out of a population of 13,000,000 were Hungarians, Germans, Ruthenians, Bulgarians and others. All three countries undertook a massive expulsion of these minorities.

The result was a criss-cross of expelees, fugitives or repatriates, some going from west to east, others from east to west. Finally, the 2,000,000 Poles repatriated from the east and the over-dense rural populations of the south of Old Poland went west to take the place of Germans expelled from the Oder region and Posnania; they themselves were replaced in the east by Lithuanians, Bielorussians and 700,000 Ukrainians. In the same way 100,000 Italians left Istria when it became part of Yugoslavia. Germans from the Sudetenland and East Prussia, both *Volksdeutsche* and *Reichsdeutsche* whose numbers may have reached 9,500,000, agglomerated in the Federal Republic, and were reinforced by those who refused to remain in the Soviet occupation zone.

These tremendous population displacements resulted in a remarkable remodelling of the ethnic and linguistic map of eastern and

central Europe. The German colonization of east European countries, which had begun at first through absorption of invaders from the east during the eighth century and had continued with the *Drang nach Osten* from the twelfth right into the eighteenth century, had been brutally crushed and the limit of Germanism forced back far towards the west. States containing a dangerous proportion of non-indigenous peoples were succeeded by states which were far more homogeneous and almost pure in nationality.

It was in Germany that the integration of these newcomers posed the most formidable economic and social problems. At first the Allies had to take charge of something like 15,000,000 human beings, the Displaced Persons Division of SHAEF repatriating 3,300,000 people and the Soviet command more than 5,000,000 prisoners (of which 732,000 were western Allied prisoners), deportees and exchange populations. Then it became the responsibility of a United Nations organ, IRO (International Refugee Organization), to deal with the refugees and DPs in German, Austrian and Italian camps; stateless people; formerly privileged persons dispossessed of their rights; political opponents; Nazi collaborators who could not or would not return to their countries of origin. A small portion of these were finally repatriated (65,000 between 1947 and 1949); the others, after

18 *Exodus*, painting by Georges Rouault (1948) ▶

16 East German refugees in a dismantled timber factory at Berlin-Neukölln, 1953

17 German cartoon on the difficulties of 'digesting' refugees from the East

political vetting and selection, were permitted to emigrate to more than eighty countries. As for the *Volksdeutsche*, they were repatriated into the Soviet, British and American occupation zones of Germany.

Thus the already dense population of a Germany reduced in area to 380,000 sq. km. was swelled by more than 10,000,000 refugees, who brought its density to 140–180 people per sq. km. Nevertheless, in spite of its paralyzed industries and the burden of the Allied occupation, Germany was able to 'digest' these 10,000,000 people. This was possible because, for the most part, they were adults and supplied a useful professional supplement, but also because the Allies restored to Germany its indispensable industrial potential.

With the exception of a 'hard core' of old people, chronic invalids, the infirm, the mentally deficient, and unemployable intellectuals, whom no selection commission would take in charge, the DPs found themselves much more easily integrated into the masses than might have been hoped, without the social disturbances and insurmountable economic difficulties which it had been feared this prodigious uprooting would produce.

THE DEMOGRAPHIC RISE

Moreover, that part of Europe which, along with the USSR, had suffered the most radical destruction, experienced the same unexpected demographic rise as the rest of the continent; and this, far from causing any crisis, was a powerful factor in economic recovery.

This population increase, which was general but unequal from country to country, was brought about by a visible, though rather slow, rise in the birth-rate and by a gradual decrease in the mortality-rate. It can be shown that the downward trend of the birth-rate, which was general for a long time in spite of the younger age at which people were marrying, was checked for several years but then slowly resumed, principally in urban zones and among the intellectually most developed social strata. On the other hand, the rate remained higher in Mediterranean Europe, which is predominantly rural; for example, southern Italy, an economically backward area, furnished two-thirds of the country's total growth between 1952 and 1953 though it comprised only 37·2 per cent of the population.

The average life-expectancy in Europe became generally longer; for women it passed 70 years in those countries which were more highly developed economically and socially (the Netherlands, Sweden, Great Britain, France), and for men it was slightly less.

Population growth was much greater in western than in eastern Europe, in spite of the clear slowing-down of the net birth-rate. Even though the loss of lives had been dreadful in eastern Europe (perhaps 20,000,000 in the USSR alone), growth was still considerable. The population of the USSR increased from 193,000,000 in 1940 to 224,000,000 in 1963; the death-rate decreased from 18·1 per thousand in 1940 to 7·3 per thousand in 1963, just as the birth-rate dropped from 31·3 per thousand in 1940 to 21·3 per thousand in 1963. Poland, which had lost between 15 and 20 per cent of its population, and 15 per cent of whose population had been affected by post-war transfers, went from a total of 15,157,000 in 1939 to 28,782,000 in 1967; Yugoslavia increased from 15,700,000 in 1948 to 19,742,000 in 1967, by which date Czechoslovakia had almost recovered its 1930 figure of 14,000,000. Rumania went from 16,113,000 to more than 19,000,000 and showed the highest rate of increase; East Germany, which rose from 15,157,000 to 17,048,000, showed the smallest.

AMERICAN AID

This massive demographic rise thus created, after a generation, an abundant reserve of workers and consumers. But Europe could not have achieved its reconstruction without recourse to either foreign aid or a foreign model. Western Europe oriented itself towards the first solution, eastern Europe towards the second. This difference can of course be explained by the difference of ideological concepts and social structure, and by the general political context of the period as well.

Since the Potsdam conference, an ever-increasing mistrust had grown up between the English-speaking countries and their capitalist neighbours, on the one hand, and the USSR (which possessed the atomic bomb from 1949) and its Communist neighbours, on the other. The Cold War was accentuated by the Truman Doctrine (12 March 1947) and further intensified by the Korean War. Communist influence was strong and capable of becoming even stronger among famished populations, still subjected to severe restrictions and threatened by unemployment. Besides, there were several incidents which demonstrated the general retreat of Europe and the reduction of the capitalist countries' forces to the defensive: Tito's victory in rejecting the British-supported king of Yugoslavia; the Greek Civil War, in which Great Britain, abandoning an undertaking that was too costly, had to call on the Americans to replace its troops; in

Asia, the victory of Communist armies over those of Chiang Kai-shek, the more or less Communist-inspired revolts in South-East Asia (Malaysia, Indo-China), and the obligation to accept the independence of India. In the eyes of the Americans, who led the western coalition, these retreats required an initiative to reverse the course of events: this was the Marshall Plan.

The objectives of this Plan were to preserve Europe from the temptation of Communism by consolidating its economy and avoiding unemployment, to exercise an irresistible attraction on the People's Democracies that were destitute of capital and essential raw materials, to create a barrier against the Communist thrust which some believed to be a military threat, and finally to create outlets for American capital and products. Europe was in fact in debt to the United States, which had sent goods and food products to its allies under the terms of 'lend-lease', and only Belgium had been able to repay its debt. The United States had been increasing its production capacity and accumulating considerable surpluses which the European states were happy to buy but for which they could not pay. The Marshall Plan certainly reflected the generous intentions of the American public, but also, incontestably, the ulterior motives of those businessmen and statesmen interested in political and economic expansion.

There was a complete synchronism between the stages of Europe's division into two blocs and mutually corresponding measures in the east and the west. The Marshall Plan was only the most spectacular and most effective of these measures. On 5 June 1947, General George C. Marshall, United States Secretary of State, proposed to the sixteen countries of Europe that they call a conference to study economic cooperation, to which the United States would offer financial aid. A committee of experts, called the Harriman Commission, presented a plan which eventually came into force in 1949. In the form of grants and loans to the European countries, the proposed aid was to open credits which would be used for purchases in the dollar area, and principally in the United States. The Organization for European Economic Cooperation (OEEC) was formed to administer this aid, and its member states agreed to facilitate inter-European trade: a European Payments Union, created in 1950, was meant to ease not only bilateral, but also multilateral payments. A parallel policy of progressive liberalization of trade was intended to stimulate investments and to increase productivity.

19 Soviet view
of Europe
collapsing under
the Marshall Plan

In view of the atmosphere of distrust that existed between the two great powers, as well as certain statements, such as Averill Harriman's report to President Truman (5 November 1947), which declared that it was important to safeguard interests measured 'not only in economic terms' but also 'strategic and political' ones, Stalin replied that the sole aim of the project was to isolate the USSR, and Foreign Minister Molotov justified his rejection of the Plan by maintaining that its establishment would inevitably make the other European states dependent on the great powers. The USSR and its allies thus refused to take part in the original conference: Yugoslavia and Bulgaria spontaneously, Poland and Czechoslovakia after having first shown willingness to accept the invitation, and ultimately Rumania and Hungary.

There can be no doubt that it was American aid which made the swift revival of the western European economy possible; it was American aid, too, which enabled Germany to effect the monetary reform that stabilized its economy and facilitated the 'German miracle'. On the other hand, American aid limited to some degree

27

the independence of benefiting governments by making it difficult for them to resist certain political pressures (such as acceptance of German rearmament) or economic ones (reduction of customs barriers; facilities for American investments and the transfer of profits to the USA; acceptance of certain more or less useful, and often unsaleable, surplus products; control by American commissions of the use of aid funds and fiscal policy, as well as industries receiving funds for re-equipment; adoption of deflationary measures; limitation of wages; competition ruinous to certain national industries; predominance of the dollar over the pound; devaluations forced on France from 1946 to 1949; stabilization of the Italian lira in 1947).

Another very serious consequence was the break – no longer solely ideological, but economic as well – between the two Europes. From 1945 all the eastern countries had developed, sometimes in substantial proportions, their trade with the west, and had become largely dependent on western countries for the provision of equipment, capital and raw materials. In the face of western integration under American direction, an integration of the Socialist countries took place under the Soviet aegis, despite difficulties caused by what was virtually a western blockade. Already ravaged by war, engaged in reorganizing themselves because of large-scale population movements and changes in economic structure required by their shift to a Socialist economy, suffering from lack of capital, the eastern countries were bound to recover much less quickly than those in the west.

THE ECONOMIC RESTORATION OF NEO-CAPITALISM

During two or three years devoted primarily to the re-establishment of communication facilities and the reconstruction of transport, production stagnated in western Europe and the level of national income rose only slowly; but then the take-off began, varying according to country and time. It will be at least useful to describe the situation – in certain respects paradoxically advantageous – of the belligerents that had suffered the greatest losses and destruction: Great Britain, Germany and the USSR.

During the war years, as Professor M. M. Postan has shown, these countries improved their industrial potential both qualitatively and quantitatively, though the degree of improvement is hard to evaluate, particularly for the USSR. Scientists, engineers, technicians, managements achieved notable progress; the governments made considerable investments in war factories which, at the end of hostilities, were

28

reconverted to the production of consumer goods. In Germany, for instance, the unremitting and spectacular bombing raids of immense Allied air fleets caused relatively little damage to the industrial war-machine. Only 20 per cent of its factories were demolished or seriously damaged. Germany had powerfully increased its production potential beyond that of 1935–39, so that its post-war capacity was hardly inferior to what it had been in 1939.

It was not until 1948 that the recovery of Europe was truly launched; from then on – apart from a few periods of relatively mild recession – progress was to be rapid, and even, in some countries, spectacular. It would be tedious to quote a mass of figures (we have an abundance of them, though they are not always comparable, particularly because of frontier changes); but a few will suffice to mark the stages and the general curve of progress. If one takes as basis the economic report for 1945–47 prepared by the Department of Economic Affairs of the United Nations, one can see that, in comparison with pre-war figures, coal production in Germany fell to 50 per cent; in Belgium, the Netherlands and Great Britain it was 89 per cent, in Italy 70 per cent of the pre-war figure. The figures for steel production were nearly the same. The only exceptions to this decline were those countries in which the German occupation had forced production to its limit (as in Silesia and Czechoslovakia, where production rose from 90 to 109 per cent) and even installed new production centres less vulnerable to Allied bombing. Only the neutral countries, notably Sweden, maintained or continued their regular progress. As for the USSR, the industrial production index fell to 58 in 1945 (100 in 1940).

In the field of agriculture the situation in Europe was more tragic: the production index (100 in 1938) was 63 in 1946, 75 in 1947. For Europe as a whole (excluding the USSR), production of fats, milk, milk products and eggs was particularly reduced. Without imports from outside Europe of manufactured or semi-manufactured goods, of coal and food products (+38 per cent), and the decrease in European exports (varying from below 30 to 50 per cent), scarcity in Europe would have been far more catastrophic than it was. Further-more, the deficit in the balance of trade became greater every year: from $2,000,000 in 1938 it leapt to $6,900,000 in 1947. The total of debts involved a deficit in the balance of payments (principally in relation to the United States) which rose to $9,000,000,000 in 1947, so that the 'dollar gap' became increasingly wide.

It was only when effective measures were put into force that recovery came about. The new capitalism, established under the spur of necessity and in imitation of the United States, presented new characteristics quite different from those of nineteenth-century monopoly capitalism. It was soon perceived that reconstruction demanded the application of such wide-ranging methods that only the state was in a position to muster the necessary capital. It was also recognized that unlimited competition could no longer be allowed to develop without control or restraint. Inspired exclusively by the search for profit, unimpeded competition leads to a waste of manpower and capital; it also encourages disregard for the development of the nation's total resources, on grounds of insufficient profitability, so that the actual needs of the population as a whole are not satisfied. Thus, willy-nilly, governments maintained and developed their role in directing the economy. In the nineteenth century it was an exception when, in the case of undertakings of national importance, the state sometimes had to take the place of defaulting private enterprise; now it became the rule. Large firms were forced to accept, and even to solicit, state intervention; they rejected it in principle but submitted to it so long as economic recovery might enable them to regain their former prosperity. In this way the state came to control, directly or otherwise, the development of national resources and the key sectors of the economy, notably sources of credit: large banks and insurance companies holding significant capital. The state also took frequent initiatives in sectors of the economy on which the nation's prosperity depended. It was not a matter of socialization, for capitalist management was maintained and every firm preserved its legal and accounting autonomy. Thus state intervention and planning – 'the most characteristic expression of the new capitalism', according to Andrew Shonfield – distinguished, in varying degrees, the new economic system.

The public sector became larger everywhere, and particularly in Italy where the state, with its multiple participations and holdings, is ubiquitous. The proportion of investment of public companies grew in total from 42 per cent in 1963 to 57 per cent in 1965 and began to level out only in 1967, even in Sweden where the Social Democratic Party, after its electoral victory in October 1960, planned to extend state control to 25 per cent of businesses. Methods were not the same everywhere; each state followed its own traditions and its particular national temperament. German reconstruction, for example, was predominantly the work of hierarchic and strongly organized professional bodies in association with powerful banks; nevertheless, the state also intervened in order to encourage certain private investments, notably in its creation of loan banks for reconstruction.

But ultimately it was the system committed, in greater or lesser degree, to planning which was most generally adopted. The most comprehensive model was the French plan: the first, called after its initiator the Monnet Plan (1946–50), has been followed by others more wide-ranging and flexible because of the use of increasingly refined techniques of national accounting. The Monnet Plan was not a case of authoritarian planning, but of a 'concerted economy'. Its character was 'indicative' in the sense that high-ranking specialists of the Commissariat du Plan and the Treasury cooperated with the heads of industrial and business firms to draw up a coherent plan, applicable to both the public and private sectors, to set medium- and long-term targets indispensable to the country's economic development, to establish production priorities, an investment programme, the rate of development and productivity, etc. The plan was not compulsory, but the state had powerful means of action, for in large part it was in control of credit through the Caisse des Dépôts (the most important French bank, which receives deposits from all the savings banks in the country, as well as pension and cooperative society funds) and the Crédit National (which controls all medium-term and a portion of long-term bank credits). The state could thus take action on the rate of interest and the amount of credit available to firms; it could impose the use of certain industrial or commercial techniques and influence the introduction of factories into certain regions. Its power was even more direct over numerous enterprises of mixed economy: it could grant subsidies, exemptions or tax rebates, loans at rates below those on the open market, by means of so-called 'fiscal contracts' that allowed it to choose the firms; and it could offer advantageous prices through the nationalized industries which provided coal, electricity, gas and transport.

Worked out by government officials and leaders of industry, without the participation of the unions or any national representation, the plan in fact offered, in Shonfield's words, 'carte blanche to the planners, the technocrats', and the large firms that had evolved it. The success that followed its adoption encouraged various other countries to use it as a model. In Great Britain, even though the country possessed very important nationalized industries, such as coal-mining and energy, it was only slowly – after several attempts at short-term planning and recourse to expedients – that the government finally adopted a five-year plan in 1962. Its response was brisker after 1964, when the prospect of entry into the European Economic Community (Common Market) led to the establishment of a National Prices and Income Board.

In Sweden, the industrial country of Europe with the highest standard of living and extremely active trade unionism, the planning role has for a long time been entrusted to the Labour Market Board. Here employers' and workers' organizations negotiate directly with a view to maintaining full employment through control of construction and investment, that is, through the selection of various industries in accordance with market fluctuations and warding off crises in them by means of a special reserve fund supported by the taxes levied on the beneficiaries. In 1962 an Economic Planning Council, presided over by the Minister of Finance, was created with the mission of forecasting essential long-term investments and subsidizing studies and projects up to 50 per cent.

For a long time the Netherlands did not have any form of planning properly speaking; the state simply exercised a direct and stringent control over salaries, and fixed ceiling prices in detail for every industrial enterprise. In 1963, however, a planning system with a five-year target was adopted.

In Federal Germany, once again the most important and active industrial state in western Europe, the regime imposed by the victors (division into 11 Länder, dissolution of the large industrial trusts and dispersion of the large banks into small units, each of whose field of activity was limited to a single Land) lasted only a few years. Since 1960 the 100 largest firms have regrouped and now employ one worker out of three; they represent more than 40 per cent of the total industrial output. And finally, the three largest banks – Deutsche Bank, Dresdner Bank and Commerz Bank – have been reconstituted. Even though Germany denies it, there exists, in addition to active state intervention, an effective planning system, but it is in the hands of the *Verband der deutschen Industrie* (Federation of German Industry) which practises, as in the Nazi era, a 'directed economy' through long-term forecast of supply and demand, and through investment planning. It is dominated by an understanding among the three large banks which, in 1960, thanks to the use of shareholders' proxies, controlled 70 per cent of the nominal value of quoted shares. Eleven banks occupied three-quarters of all seats on the *Aufsichtsräte*, or company Supervisory Boards (the three large banks occupying more than half), which keep a close watch on managers' activities. By means of this centralization, the banks intervene in industrial enterprises, imposing agreements on them to avoid all competition and closely controlling their investments. Close to each minister there is also a *Beirat* (advisory council) which maintains permanent contacts between industry and the administration. Finally, the state, within the framework of social security (housing, health), education and transport, assists basic industries through public investments, reduction of taxes, and subsidies; it does the same for shipbuilding, agriculture and exports. Dr Ludwig Erhard, Chancellor from 1963 to 1966, took this path in March 1964 – after having rejected it up to then – by creating a five-member Council of Economic Experts. Thus, to quote Shonfield again, 'the basic institutional elements necessary to a systematic economic plan' were brought together.

In Italy there existed from before the war a very important public and semi-public sector as well as state-controlled monopolistic enterprises. ENI (Ente Nazionale Idrocarburi) was directed for a long time by the powerful Enrico Mattei; IRI (Istituto per la Ricostruzione Industriale), comprising 140 companies, controls through its affiliates half the production of steel, shipping and certain banks. The state also owns 86 per cent of the capital of the Banca Nazionale del Lavoro (the most important commercial bank) and the total capital of the Banco di Napoli and the Cassa dei Depositi e Prestiti (comparable to the French Caisse des Dépôts, though less important). Credit control is exercised by an interministerial committee of credit, composed of the ministers themselves; it confirms or rejects every important request for credit – in the private or public sector – granted by the banks under the control of the Banca d'Italia. It is the latter which vigorously encourages exports and directs credits towards the establishment of growth points in the regions of underemployment: central and southern Italy and the Veneto. After having restricted itself for a long time to private or regional plans, Italy finally rallied in 1957 to the policy of comprehensive planning.

MONETARY REFORMS

After the war, Europe found itself with a great abundance of paper money at the same time that it was suffering a dearth of primary products. This superabundance of debased currency for which there was no use caused a substantial fall in buying power: 50 per cent in Great Britain and Switzerland. In West Germany this decline was catastrophic, and there was a return to barter, the unit of value being the cigarette (4 to 5 Marks). No government had the courage to proceed rapidly with the necessary measures of currency reform, except for Belgium, where the Finance Minister A. Gutt re-established parity with the dollar (50 Belgian francs) by reducing the amount of money in circulation through exchange of notes and blocking of accounts. When this reform was proposed in France by Pierre Mendès-France, General de Gaulle turned it down. Thus France was saddled with financial instability, from which it did not emerge until 1958, when the new franc was created with a value of approximately 5 to the dollar. In Greece the same disastrous policy led in 1953 to creation of a new drachma with a fixed value of 2,000 to the pound. By controlling credits and raising the discount rate, Norway and Sweden arrested inflation. Only one large country copied Gutt's example, much later, with spectacular success: Federal Germany which, in 1948, replaced the 95 per cent devalued Reichsmark by the Deutsche Mark. Great Britain experienced serious difficulties in this regard, and in 1949, then again in 1967, had to devalue the pound – followed by sixteen countries which are tied to Britain by very close economic relations.

These divergent policies and the exchange controls which were maintained for a long time constituted a great restraint on international trade. In 1957 an attempt was made to create an international capital market by taking advantage of certain unused cash balances; banks of issue or of commerce and the International Monetary Fund placed a part of their dollar resources, in the form of short-term deposits, in banks outside United States territory (where interest rates were low). Loans financed in this way are formulated in dollars (Euro-dollars), but they could be made in any other currency. They facilitate international, and even internal, transactions since they convert foreign currency holdings into national currency; Euro-money already plays an important role and appears as a remedy for the inflation which is not without danger for the future. In any case this embryo of an international currency reinforces the hegemony of the dollar.

20, 21 Nationalized industries: the National Coal Board in Britain and a Renault plant in France

Planning is not the only novel aspect of the new industrial society; nationalization is another means of increasing direct state participation in production.

Even before 1939, left-wing parties in numerous countries had regarded it as irrational and unjust that the national wealth and key sectors of the economy, or industries working for national defence, should be monopolized for the profit of private groups. Just after the liberation, the industries in France which had passed into the hands of the Germans and those that had voluntarily worked for the occupying forces were nationalized: in 1944 these were the coal mines, the Renault factories, the Gnôme et Rhône motor company, the gas and electricity industries, the principal deposit banks and

35

22 Nationalization as a street-circus; by a French Sunday painter

insurance companies. In Great Britain, between 1946 and 1949, coal mines, railroads, civil aviation, electricity, gas and the Bank of England were all nationalized, as well as the steel industry (de-nationalized by the Conservatives and *re*-nationalized under the Labour Government in 1967). In Austria, German firms were nationalized, and also those seized by the Soviets during their occupation (24 per cent of industrial production). This happened in Norway, too, in the case of mines and large hydroelectric enterprises, the Aardal aluminium plants and the Moi-i-Rama foundries. A comparable case is the Spanish mixed enterprise, INF (Instituto Nacional de Industria).

ELECTRONICS

The industrial production of Europe, like that of the rest of the world, is also in the process of being completely transformed by the advent of automation and electronics, which have been penetrating

36

23 The unavoidable computer ▶

all techniques of industry, transport and commerce. Since the beginning of the century automatism has made its appearance, and in 1945 automation was no longer a novelty. Electronics, on the other hand, introduced a radical change in every field. Leaving aside its role in medicine, biology and astronomy (e.g. the electronic microscope and telescope), as well as its practical application in telecommunications and the regulation of sea and air transport, we need only observe that it has completely changed manufacturing techniques and the physical appearance of factories, which it empties – in the full sense of the word – of their personnel. Electronics make automation more flexible than other forms of mechanized production, for electronic regulation can adapt the speed of a machine to the material on which it works. Electronic devices are capable of correcting errors by immediately recognizing a defective piece and rejecting it ('feedback'), and of carrying out work more quickly and with greater precision. Administration is also facilitated by computers and electronic calculators in study-centres (statistics, planning) or accounting offices (invoicing, daily stocktaking), in banks or in postal chequeing services (GIRO), as well as in research laboratories.

The results of such a discovery are by now considerable. It forces the replacement of costly, outdated and unprofitable machinery by equipment which can be acquired only by firms disposing of large capital. This has precipitated the move towards concentration of companies which is accelerating before our eyes and arouses, as a counterpart, the disquiet of administrative staffs (the first to be threatened) and skilled workers whose qualifications assure them relatively high salaries. It results in the dismissal of supernumerary staff, and also requires the lengthy and difficult training of highly qualified personnel, capable of improving the delicate equipment or simply ensuring its maintenance. It makes basic or technological research a vital obligation for any country that wishes to remain in the vanguard of industrial progress and material power. And this research requires very powerful financial means, large groups of experts working in teams, and exceedingly expensive materials. It cannot be achieved without government subsidies: the USSR government provides the total, the American 75 per cent.

CONCENTRATION OF INDUSTRY: THE DOMINATION OF BANKS

Another characteristic of the modern economy is, on the one hand, the creation of giant industries concentrated much more according to a management plan and financial control than a properly technical and geographic programme; and, on the other hand, the increasing influence of banking capitalism on industrial capitalism – although self-financing is becoming increasingly important, notably in France and Italy. This concentration does not always appear clearly: in Germany, for example, it was much more marked in the steel and coal industries in 1935 (57 per cent of coal and 95 per cent of raw steel) than in 1958 (30 and 78 per cent; perhaps 85 per cent for steel in 1963); and one can see the same phenomenon in the chemical and electrical industries. But many of the small or medium-sized industries which survive have only a façade of independence; they are no more than sub-contractors making products which the large firms find it more advantageous to have them supply. Besides, their separate existence is often only apparent and has been rectified by financial links created by the banks which control them.

The concentration predicted by Marx has thus become a fact, though it is less marked in Europe than in the United States. As Jean Meynaud shows in the preface to his study of this problem in Belgium, *Mythologie des groupes financiers*, 'It constitutes [through the relationships it establishes among businesses] one of the original elements, varying in intensity according to country and section, of modern capitalism. It is one of the essential aspects of this vast process of regrouping economic units, the result of which is to place the important decisions of industrial life under the control of a private oligarchy.' And J. Houssiaux points out that 'The 975 administrators of the hundred largest financial firms in France have more than a thousand personal links with other companies through shares.'

This concentration can be explained by the need to find larger markets and, for that reason, to produce by more profitable methods (e.g. serial manufacture, reduction of overheads, merger of planning offices). It is also caused by the need for capital, which large firms obtain more easily than small ones. Already begun (and particularly advanced in Germany) before 1940, the movement towards concentration accelerated when the Common Market appeared to be going into full force; this encouraged firms to become as competitive as possible. We find concentration principally in the most dynamic industries: chemicals, electricity, electronics.

Thus were created giant corporations, of which the Société Générale of Belgium offers a particularly characteristic example. It dominates practically the whole of the Belgian economy: in 1959 it had under its control from 50 to 80 per cent of bank deposits, more than 60 per cent of insurance companies, 70 per cent of the trade in ferrous metals, more than 40 per cent of the iron and steel industry, 30 per cent of coal, 25 per cent of electrical energy. In the same way the two largest German companies, which in 1954 controlled 37–38 per cent of the production of the electromechanical industries and 72–91 per cent of refineries and coal conversion, account for 40 per cent of national industrial production, with one-third of the industrial work-force. The production of sheet-iron in Great Britain, before the creation of the British Steel Corporation, was concentrated in five firms which manufactured in 1963 three times as much as the fifty firms that existed in 1937; in the tinplate industry two powerful firms produce more than the thirty-four in operation in 1937. In Italy, too, the merger of Edison and Montecatini created one of the most important chemical groups in the world. In Sweden mergers and regroupings have been as numerous since 1966 as during the whole of the eighteen preceding years.

These giant combines are far from having reached their final form; there are still frequent mutations. One of their most remarkable traits is the diversification of their activities and investments. Prudent leaders of such enterprises do not limit their activity to a single product which, as the result of some discovery or technical innovation, runs the risk – almost from one day to the next – of no longer finding customers.

These concentrations are effected either through a simple merger between two or more businesses which create in common a new enterprise or mutual subsidiaries, or through the absorption or control by one firm of another, most often by means of new joint investments or the establishment of analysis and research laboratories or distribution services.

Intensified since 1963, the movement has become general. In 1966 alone, as many mergers took place throughout the world as during all the ten preceding years. Before 1963 no French firm figured among the 500 largest industrial firms of the world, today there are 23; Great Britain accounts for 55, Germany 30, Italy 8.

IMPROVEMENTS IN INDUSTRIAL PRODUCTION

Since 1945 there has not been a really serious economic crisis – only recessions of short duration, fluctuations, as Shonfield puts it, 'rather than reverses in the curve'. These have been due not to overproduction, as used to be thought, but to the more rapid growth of demand than production. It would be wrong not to mention also the role played in this disappearance of serious crises by economists who learned how to put into practice methods that could avoid over-production while maintaining full employment and the level of demand and investment.

By the time reconstruction was completed along its main lines around 1952, the pre-war level of production had been surpassed and productive capacity was in full use. Whereas the average annual growth rate in western Europe was 1·7 per cent during the period 1920–37 and nearly 3·5 per cent between 1948 and 1963, it has been more than doubled in all these countries since 1963. Maurice Niveau comments that 'the record of growth seems historically without precedent.' However, all the European countries have not been capable of progress at the same pace. Niveau classifies them according to rapid (West Germany, Italy) or slow growth (Norway, Denmark, Sweden, Belgium, Great Britain); we may also distinguish an inter-mediate category which would include Switzerland, the Netherlands and France.

The results were remarkable; in the twelve countries of western Europe, not only did the productivity rate double (3·5 per cent during the 1950s), but also unemployment virtually vanished even though the population was increasing. Full employment was achieved, and there was even a shortage of labour in the leading western European countries which brought a great influx of workers from North Africa, Italy, Spain, Portugal, Greece and Turkey. Certain countries (Switzer-land in particular) even found themselves inundated by foreign workers without the least objection from the national trade unions.

Between 1954 and 1961 the countries with the most dynamic industries – Germany, Italy, France, Switzerland – stood out, while the laggards were Belgium and Great Britain. Then in 1962 a period of recession began in certain countries; the threat of inflation in Italy and France put a brake on domestic consumption and investment, so that in 1963 the rate of expansion dropped in Italy and remained stagnant in France. Switzerland and Sweden now showed the highest growth rate in Europe (6 per cent), and Belgium detached itself from the group at the rear to leap into third or fourth place with a rate of 5·5 per cent. The only country which remained consistently in the last position was Great Britain with an average annual growth rate of 2·5 per cent. As a basis of comparison it may be noted that the gross national product (in dollars) of Japan, which has become the second economic power in the world, increased by 92 per cent, after the United States (38 per cent), between 1964 and 1967; West Germany followed with an increase of 27 per cent (though it continued in third place), then Great Britain with 31 per cent (fourth), France with 34 per cent (fifth) and Italy (sixth) with 44 per cent.

AGRICULTURAL PRODUCTION

It is perhaps in the agricultural sphere that the face of western Europe has undergone the most profound changes. The traditional peasant economy has completely altered its character, particularly during the most recent years. The farm cultivated only by members of one family, the ideal of which was to be self-sufficient and to seek in one local or regional market the monetary resources necessary to cover its needs, has disappeared; a market economy has willy-nilly replaced a subsistence economy. Almost everywhere, and not only in those countries that are technologically most advanced, this profound change has taken place with astonishing speed. It was brought about by extensive mechanization. Tractors and agricultural machinery, which barely existed in significant quantities before 1939, except in Great Britain, have multiplied, notably since 1948, in France, Germany, and all the rest of Europe; these are sometimes smaller models, particularly adapted to the small tracts where they are often used. The use of fertilizers and insecticides increased 85 per cent between 1939 and 1959, almost doubling the pre-war figures. The improvement of seed has been general, as has that of animal-feed; this, together with artificial insemination, has led to an increase in the number of farm animals. The use of new feeding methods and the stimulation of egg-laying have increased the output of poultry. Finally, there has been a scientific, and no longer empirical, specialization of cultivation, aided by the facilities of commercialization.

Other factors, the same as those operative in industry, have also played a part: the memory of scarcity and privations endured during the war, the increase of a more demanding urban population, the growth of investment either by the *bourgeois* of neighbouring towns or by the government, as in France, southern Italy and Great Britain. The result has been a spectacular increase in productivity, sometimes even more rapid than industrial growth. In 1962, total agricultural production in western Europe surpassed the pre-war total by 30 per cent, so that the whole region, with the exception of Great Britain,

24 Advertisement of the
British Egg Marketing Board

25 Factory-type egg farm in
Western Germany

was 95 per cent self-sufficient in cereals and was even in a position to export potatoes, vegetables and milk products.

This increase in production, which of course did not occur equally everywhere, had the same effects as in nineteenth-century Great Britain and in the United States at the beginning of the twentieth century: an exodus from the country to the towns and a great structural transformation through the disappearance of no longer viable units. Already started at the beginning of the century, this process accelerated to the point where the peasant has been completely changed into a producer for the market. This raises the problems of how to use these uprooted populations and of the social imbalance which they cause.

43

European agriculture remains important, even if its relative role in the economic life of each country may be receding – except for the southern part of the continent where serious underemployment continues to exist. The proportion of the total population, decreasing everywhere, which devotes itself to farming is between 10 and 20 per cent in most countries: 40 per cent in southern Europe as compared with less than 5 per cent in Great Britain and Sweden, and between 5 and 10 per cent in France, Belgium, the Netherlands, Switzerland and West Germany. Of the working population, agriculture still engages 25 per cent. The rural exodus is extremely important and has many causes, principally the exiguity of no longer profitable farms: smallholdings disappear one after the other, giving way to more substantial farms provided with capital to obtain the means needed to increase productivity. Nevertheless, all governments, recognizing the electoral power of the peasant masses, protect their agriculture in varying degrees, thus encouraging the increase of productivity. They also support high prices, which make European agriculture less competitive and create surpluses of certain products that are not only difficult to export but sometimes have to be destroyed in order to avoid a drop in market prices. However, one must note the example of Great Britain, whose agriculture is almost unique in Europe (only the Netherlands and Denmark approach it at all): agricultural production there is paradoxically one of the country's most prosperous activities whereas only 3·5 per cent of the working population is devoted to it. In many sectors its productivity is remarkable: in 1964 its yield per hectare (approximately $2\frac{1}{2}$ acres) was higher than that of France by 25 per cent for wheat and barley, 35 per cent for potatoes, an average of 33 per cent for milk cows, almost 70 per cent for sugar beet. This progress has been achieved by means of massive government subsidies, granted mainly to 'commercial' farms, that is, in proportion to their productivity and efficiency. Only 200,000 farms require full-time work; 55 per cent of the farmers own their own land, the rest being tenants. Government subsidies are so important that, as C. Moindrot writes, 'British agricultural revenue would be cut 80 per cent if public aid were reduced.' This is doubtless the example others must try to follow.

In 1944, when its territory was liberated, and in 1945, after the return of its prisoners of war, the USSR confronted a gigantic task of reconstruction, with 20,000,000 dead (mostly men between 20 and 45), a million of whom had perished of starvation in Leningrad. To these must be added a considerable deficit of births. The industrial potential was no more than one-fifth or one-quarter of what it had been formerly. The losses were as heavy in the agricultural as in the industrial sphere, and the life of the nation depended, by more than a third, on imports from the United States. The reconstruction drive, though comparable to the one Lenin had imposed in 1921, was nevertheless much more rapid; the rhythm of previous development was accelerated by orientating the main effort towards basic industries. On the other hand, the German advance had caused the transfer of many industries to the east and Siberia; these continued to develop while the great centres destroyed by the western invasion were reconstructed and expanded.

By 1953, left to its own forces and resources, the USSR was able, through its fierce energy, to attain its pre-war level and to increase its industrial production. In addition, its population grew in a rhythm comparable to that of North America, but more slowly than before the war. It is estimated that, from 208,000,000 in 1959, its population increased to 233,000,000 in July 1966 – and 180,000,000 of these had been born after the October Revolution of 1917.

The Soviet economy had been consistently dominated by planning ever since 1928, but there were important changes. In proportion to the increasing number and diversity of enterprises, the economy acquired a more complex character, and the centralization of direction in the hands of Gosplan, with its extensive bureaucracy, caused waste and an intolerable loss of time. A profound reform, made possible by Stalin's death in 1953, was begun in 1955 and went into full effect in 1957. It aimed to cross 'the threshold of modernization', that is, to satisfy consumers' demands for greater comfort, to allow a devolution of the direction of factories and decentralize their organization by means of regional economic councils. Such was the object of an ephemeral reform (it disappeared in 1965), which created 105 *Sovnarkhoz* charged with administration of the economy on a regional scale and with playing the role of intermediary in trade between the different regions.

45

The new reform of 1965, inspired by the ideas of the economist Yevsei Libermann, consists of 'stimulating the plan'; a special bank directs long-term investment towards priority sectors of the economy and regulates prices. The novelty of the reform is the central role attributed to the profitability of individual concerns, that is, the profit they realize as the result of increasing their productivity and sales. The profit made by each concern serves to finance development of productive capacity and to maintain funds for social services, as well as to give efficient managers a bonus instead of, as previously, a straight salary. This 'incentive' fund was created by the management in agreement with the trade unions. Planning and incentive were thus organically linked in the same system. The enterprise also saw its responsibilities extended; it had financial autonomy and was required to finance its working capital through bank credits; it established direct relations with its suppliers and the retail shops with which it formed a contractual association. In cases of fundamental disagreement, the central ministry arbitrated.

According to Pierre-Louis Reynaud, 'the present mechanisms do not constitute a return to capitalism'. Rather, it is a new type of economy reflecting a new economic theory which is taking shape step by step, for the imperatives of technology and human needs are the same at analogous levels of development; hence the economy must respond to the vital contradiction between the growing need for human liberty, on the one hand, and the constraints of a technology that cannot be effective without strong organization, on the other. Its aim must be to combine freedom and direction. This is basically the problem which is posed identically in all developed countries, and the future of reform, in the USSR as elsewhere, depends on the quality of the directors placed at the head of enterprises. It is a case of neither 'petit-bourgeois reformism', as the Maoists describe it, nor 'neo-capitalism', as certain western polemicists maintain; it is still a planned production system organized to respond to collective requirements. Not a kopeck of profits can be invested by individuals for the purpose of personal gain, since private ownership of the means of production no longer exists.

The enterprises to which the reform has been applied have increased their profits by 25 per cent; since the average national increase has been 10 per cent, this proves that the greater increase is due much more to the growth of production than to that of sales volume (+10 per cent). Incentives have made it possible for credits allotted

26 Cartoon in *Krokodil* against the independent peasant resisting collectivization

27 Aerial view of an automobile factory on the Volga

28 The rouble strengthened by industrialization

to social and cultural activities to increase by 80 per cent, those for housing construction by 50 per cent. Gradually extended to new types of businesses – not only large industry but also small local industries (e.g. construction, retail trade), the creation of incentive funds has been successful mainly in the pilot shops where the experiment began. The insufficiencies recorded in 1967 were attributed to the fact that the system was not yet in full force everywhere: certain businesses which adopted the new methods of direction were linked, for their supplies and sales, to others which were still faithful to the old system. Moreover, certain ministries were reluctant to give up their habit of intervening in the functioning of enterprises.

THE NEW ORGANIZATION OF THE PEOPLE'S DEMOCRACIES

Having passed over into the Socialist camp as a result of their liberation by the Soviet army, the eastern European countries naturally show a quite different evolution from that of the USSR, whose point of departure in 1945 was totally dissimilar.

The experience of planning and the prestige of the victory it had won enabled the USSR to proceed with a relatively rapid reconstruction of the new people's republics. Overpopulated (with the exception of Czechoslovakia), their frontiers everywhere in disorder, they had to begin with a complete change in their political and social structure and a transformation of their economy; then, after rejecting the Marshall Plan, they undertook an extensive reconversion of their industries and patterns of trade.

At the outbreak of the war, all these countries, excepting Yugoslavia, Bulgaria and part of Czechoslovakia, were still by and large under a régime of estate-owners, in which a few thousand absentee landlords lorded it over a mass of agricultural workers or ignorant and poor smallholders. Industries and natural resources were in the hands of companies controlled by foreign banks; it was still a semi-colonial system dominated by France and Germany. In 1939, the latter – the principal client – had finally succeeded in creating a German-controlled Mitteleuropa, the destruction of which became possible upon the defeat of Hitler.

In the first period of reorganization from 1945 to 1948, the properties and firms which had come under German 'protection' (notably the Hermann Goering Works), and those of nationals compromised by their collaboration with the occupying power, were nationalized. In Slovakia, the Hungarians and Germans were expropriated without compensation, and enterprises such as the Skoda Works in Pilsen were 'made ours', i.e. became community property; this was true also of the oil wells in Rumania. During the same period banks, insurance companies, sources of power, mines, metallurgy, and all large industrial firms were nationalized; similar measures were adopted in Albania after the Italian defeat, and in Poland in the case of factories employing more than fifty workers. It was only in 1948 and 1949 that this took place, in stages, in Rumania and Hungary.

At the same time, the governments of these countries undertook the reform which was most urgent in the eyes of the masses: agricultural reform. After some hesitant attempts – particularly an excessive and hastily executed division of land, which multiplied the number of smallholdings (on the principle that 'the land belongs to the man who cultivates it') – the reform had the result of transferring, in Bulgaria, some 475,000 acres from the Church and the monasteries to communes and small farmers; in this way nearly 15,000,000 acres in Poland, more than 5,000,000 in Czechoslovakia, nearly 5,000,000 in Hungary, 3,500,000 in Rumania and nearly 2,000,000 acres in Yugoslavia passed into the hands of agricultural workers and state farms. In East Germany 8,000,000 acres of arable land and forest were divided among poor peasants and refugees, or became state property. Everywhere the overturning of the old agrarian structure went deep. The land was either taken over by the state, or distributed among smallholders in lots of about 12 acres each.

Thus in almost all parts of eastern Europe, except for Poland, there now exist, along with individual farms (which are less and less numerous and persist primarily in mountainous regions), two agricultural sectors. One is public, formed of state farms, which are large holdings obtaining good yields with the aid of strongly mechanized equipment. The other sector is cooperative; there are three or four types with local variations (e.g. the LPG – Landwirtschaftliche Produktionsgenossenschaften – in East Germany), ranging from the farm still based on private ownership of the soil to one that is almost entirely socialized. One type is the association of farms, each of which retains ownership of its animals and the limits of whose lands are still marked by boundaries; here the most important work is undertaken in common by making use of cooperative machinery and that which is lent by state equipment stations. In a second type, boundaries disappear and there is a collective rotation of crops; but cattle-raising remains with the individual farmer and the profits are distributed in proportion to the extent of land owned by each cooperating farm. In a third type, we find all the means of production (including livestock) collectivized, each family retaining a parcel of land for its own use; profits are distributed in proportion to the work furnished by its members. Finally, there is the real *kolkhoz*, in which the profits are divided according to the quantity and quality of each man's labour.

The development of this agrarian revolution has been uneven; it has been abandoned and even reversed, when peasant opposition appeared. In East Germany it was resumed in a decisive way in 1958; by 1965, 986,000 peasants were members of agricultural and market-garden cooperatives which farmed 85·7 per cent of all cultivated land, in addition to 6·7 per cent developed by large public holdings. Thus practically all arable land in the Democratic Republic is socialized.

In Rumania, agricultural collectivization was completed in 1962, by which date only 6 per cent of farmland formed the private sector, whereas the collective sector comprised state farms (5,000,000 acres) and agricultural production cooperatives (24,000,000 acres). In

Czechoslovakia, state farms, located mainly in the repopulated regions after the departure of the Sudeten Germans, occupy 21 per cent of agricultural land (3,700,000), collective farms 11,250,000 acres, and individual farms – principally in Slovakia – less than 1,500,000. Collectivization in Hungary, reorganized in 1956, was not completed until 1961, when 93 per cent of farmland was cultivated by 333 state farms on one-ninth of the soil, and by 4,566 cooperatives cultivating the remainder. The members of the cooperatives also retain a fair extent of private parcels since these supply an important part of the rice, meat, milk and egg markets.

It is Poland which has the least socialized agriculture of the People's Democracies and which encountered the most active resistance to collectivization. In 1962 the socialized sector (cooperatives and large state farms) had no more than 2,500,000 members cultivating 13 per cent of the soil (of which only 2 per cent comprised the cooperatives), as against 3,000,000 individual farms cultivating 87 per cent of the soil. Their yields are small (less than 2,000 kilos in the cooperative

29 Poster showing agricultural and industrial production in East Germany

30 Modern methods of peat-cutting in Hungary

farms). With a rapidly rising birth-rate, Poland suffers from excess density in its rural population; there is too much underemployment even in the state farms (13 workers per 250 acres), and in the private sector employment is at the rate of 40–50 workers per 250 acres. Productivity is low, but the country can supply its own needs.

Industrial growth and – in the case of certain People's Democracies – the beginning of industrialization both took place rapidly. East Germany, also adopting the criterion of profitability, has become one of the top industrial powers of Europe (sixth – and tenth in the world); it leads all the east European countries, immediately behind the USSR, with 65·6 per cent of its working population employed in industry, home crafts, trade and transport. It plays a leading role in the affairs of Comecon. When the division of Germany, in May 1949, resulted in the split of the country into two distinct parts, East Germany had to organize its economy in such a way as to assure its independence of the west. By 1952 reconstruction was completed; a series of plans and, since 1964, a 'perspective plan' of seven years have organized a new economy which increasingly distinguishes the two Germanies. Since 1956 there has been every reason, so far as East Germany is concerned, to speak of a 'pan-German miracle'. It was the country's good fortune to possess important deposits of lignite which, because of its low caloric power, was useless until 1951 when Georg Bilkenroth and Erich Rammler discovered a method of converting it so as to produce metallurgical coke for use in the powerful combine of Schwarze Pump. In addition, the process discovered by Säuberlich, Baake and Lux made it possible, with the use of furnaces of only 3 metres height, to exploit ores poor in iron and too acid to be treated in the classical high furnaces. The lignite (of which East Germany is the number-one producer in the world) used in these low furnaces and in carbochemicals also furnishes 90 per cent of electrical power. The metallurgical and machine industries predominate; a very important chemical industry has been developed; while at the same time the world reputation of East Germany's optical, photographic equipment and allied industries has been maintained. As for atomic energy, a beginning has been made in East Germany as a result of uranium deposits exploited by Wismuth, a Soviet-German company with its centre near Karl-Marx Stadt. East Germany suffers from a labour shortage: 2,609,000 workers, attracted by higher salaries, went over to the west between 1950 and 1961 (as against 424,000 who returned from West Germany). Many of these

31, 32 The Berlin Wall from the west; and an East German poster showing Western Germany, weighed down by a nuclear missile, losing the economic race

were specialized workers and technicians trained at great expense, forming a highly qualified cadre attracted by the high salaries of the west and the United States.

Like East Germany, Czechoslovakia is a highly industrialized country, particularly Bohemia, Silesia (Slezsko) and part of Moravia. At present there is a drive to industrialize Slovakia, in order to abolish any disparity between the two major parts of the Republic.

Poland, the largest and most populous of the People's Democracies, is less industrialized than its neighbours, East Germany and Czechoslovakia, although it has abundant and varied natural resources (coal, iron ore, zinc, lead, salt). Its industry is entirely socialized and, in spite of showing rapid growth, still occupied no more than one-third of the working population in 1967.

Even before 1914, Hungary was no longer a purely agricultural state. The object of its first three-year plan (1947–49) was the development of its plentiful aluminium deposits and the manufacture of heavy machinery and machine tools. Its present orientation favours

53

the chemical and plastics industries, fine instruments, bus production and aeronautics.

Finally, Rumania emerged in 1945 from a state of underdevelopment, with a largely peasant population (four-fifths of the population); it had exported cereals, but its important mineral resources (gas, oil, manganese, lead, copper and bauxite) were exploited by foreign companies. After nationalization in 1948, the country turned towards heavy industry, the manufacture of machinery and a large petrochemical and wood industry. More than half the firms are in the hands of the state; the rest are local or cooperative enterprises. The rhythm of growth in Rumania has been the most rapid of all the Socialist countries, with a consistent acceleration and an average growth rate of 10 per cent from 1950 to 1965. Rumania has also had the highest average annual productivity rate of all these countries: 8·7 per cent from 1959 to 1965.

Except for Rumania, the development of all the People's Democracies has been irregular; several have had to revise their plans along the way, even to abandon them sometimes and take a pause. In

33 The Kralupy Chemical Works in Czechoslovakia

34, 35 Polish poster (1949) promoting the six-year plan; and a petrochemical plant in Plock, Poland

general, they have had to slow down their effort since 1962. In Poland in 1964, the national gross product per capita was a third of that of France, barely more than half of that of Czechoslovakia, slightly less than a third of that of East Germany.

What are the reasons for these setbacks? In Czechoslovakia it is the labour shortage, the delay in the development of power and transport equipment; in Poland, the unwillingness of underemployed agricultural workers to take up work in mining and industry; in Hungary, dependence on foreign sources for raw materials and power, three-quarters of which are imported. A cause common to all these countries is the rigidity of planning, which leaves little room for initiative.

YUGOSLAVIA

Among the Communist states of central and eastern Europe, Yugoslavia has a place apart; since 1948 its evolution has been different from that of the other eastern countries. At the time of its liberation,

55

achieved by the Yugoslavs themselves under Tito's leadership – the Soviet army helping at the last moment to complete the German débâcle – Yugoslavia was completely devastated by war operations, decimated by losses in battle, civil war, massacres of population, prisoners of war and hostages. But even before the complete elimination of the Germans, a federal government had been established, under the leadership of the Communist Party, which had sketched out the reorganization of the country. In a land where large estates did not exist, all the properties belonging to conquered foreigners (mostly German and Hungarian) or to nationals who had collaborated with the occupying forces were confiscated on behalf of the state; then, in 1946 and 1948, it was the turn of the greater part of industry. After the end of 1947, the public sector extended to 100 per cent of bank workers; 80 per cent of workers in industry, which was still little developed; and only 3 per cent of agricultural workers. As in the other People's Democracies, the private sector dominated in small industry, home industries and agriculture, though agricultural production cooperatives already existed.

The government worked out a reconstruction plan, faithfully modelled after the Soviet plans; it was most ambitious, but it forecast a rate of growth which the Soviets themselves considered too rapid

36 Ironworks at Jesenice, Yugoslavia

and which required very large investments. The strong nationalism that had nourished the Yugoslavs' self-achieved victory was behind this insufficiently realistic plan; its application, however, was pursued with determination, in a spirit of independence that was demonstrated in the rejection of Marshall aid and also of any Soviet interference. The consequence was a break with the USSR and a ban on the country by the Socialist states, which subjected Yugoslavia to an exceedingly vigorous blockade. At the same time, the lack of technicians and financial resources needed for the plan and for social changes resulted, in 1951, in a catastrophic delay in its fulfilment. Tito then had to turn towards the western countries, while remaining faithful to Socialism and making no major ideological concession to the new conditions in which he was placed by the rupture with the east. Up until 1951–52, efforts to fulfil the plan continued, the collectivization of agriculture was accelerated, nationalization expanded, etc.; but as failure became evident, it was necessary to revise a certain number of the plan's provisions.

Thus arose a new Marxism, whose aim was to achieve Socialism while assuring maximum freedom to the function of economic laws and the maximum of Socialist democracy. Workers' management was established by a law of 1950, and the cooperatives were reorganized in 1953. It was a matter of replacing state capitalism and bureaucratic tendencies by workers' self-administration. Workers' councils, chosen by the personnel, manage their factories through the intermediary of a committee. On this committee sits a director – the representative and nominee of the state – who sees to the normal running of the plant; the committee has to approve payments and balance-sheets, and the distribution of the portion of capital left to the factory's disposition. As for the plan, it is developed by a committee which works under the Committee for the National Economy, a subdivision of the federal executive council which represents the state.

The new organization of agriculture abolished the collectivization forced through between 1947 and 1953. The cooperatives, divided into the four classical types already mentioned, numbered 6,994 in 1951 and cultivated 20 per cent of arable land. After the droughts of 1950 and 1952, they were dissolved at the discretion of their members, who were permitted to withdraw individually; their number fell to 2,500 in 1953. The corrective applied to avoid a revival of capitalism in farming was the limitation of individual properties to 25 acres;

the remainder was confiscated for the benefit of the state farms against an eventual indemnification.

The economic situation improved fairly rapidly as a result. But since 1965 there has been a grave crisis in the balance of payments; rapid inflation and the rise in prices and salaries have forced devaluation of the dinar. At the beginning of 1968 the situation seemed to have been corrected: the dinar and prices were stabilized, agricultural production had made progress, and it was no longer necessary for Yugoslavia to import wheat. Nevertheless, economic growth has not recovered its impetus, perhaps because of increasing inequality among the various republics of the federation. Montenegro, Bosnia and Macedonia, the poor and underdeveloped regions, whose standard of living has remained low, are hostile to the customs policy which they consider too liberal to imports; the richer republics, on their side, demand a reduction in the role of the federal government and retrenchments in the federal budget which, in their eyes, principally benefits the poor republics.

BULGARIA AND ALBANIA
The part of the Balkan peninsula which belongs to the Mediterranean zone includes two People's Democracies – Bulgaria and Albania –

37 Primitive agricultural methods in Albania

38 Hydroelectric dam under construction in Bulgaria

but only the former belongs to Comecon since the schism between the USSR and China. This region suffers from drought, its soil is in large part mountainous and its subsoil poor in minerals; its people, who are particularly backward, live in miserable conditions. Albania, which existed until 1945 under a feudal regime, is riven by fierce feuds among rival clans and is virtually isolated. Bulgaria, where even before the war cooperative farming was the rule, is essentially a rural country, with a public sector of several large collective farms on the Soviet model; but 71 per cent of families, occupying 85 per cent of arable land, are grouped in production cooperatives. In industry, where insurance companies were nationalized in 1947, the private sector comprises only home crafts and traders, who account for 5 per cent of productive capacity. Successive plans have concentrated on the modernization of agriculture, but drought and resistance to collectivization have made their execution slow. The most recent plan aims at the development of citrus fruits, vines, olive trees and tobacco, the principal exports to the USSR and the other People's Democracies which, on their side, supply consumers' products, machines and textiles.

59

Apart from those remaining outside the two blocs which have confronted each other since 1947 – Sweden and Finland in the north, Albania which became pro-Chinese and left the eastern bloc, Spain and Portugal whose dictatorial regimes exclude them from the group of liberal states – the various countries of Europe have, for political and economic reasons, regrouped or attempted to regroup. It has been a matter of tightening, on the economic plane, the cohesion of states that are bound together through their military alliances – the North Atlantic Treaty Organization (NATO, 1949) and the Warsaw Pact (1955) – or by ideology or a common economic system. Thus originated the EEC and Comecon, both tending towards economic integration, for the problems are identical in east and west, industrial civilization making it necessary everywhere to construct larger economic groups within which it is easier to expand, to remodel and to harmonize the conditions of production and consumption. But if the objectives are more or less admittedly the same, the mechanisms put into use are strikingly different.

The Common Market (EEC) and The European Free Trade Association (EFTA)
We know the objectives of the Marshall Plan: in the short term, restoration of the economy, and, in the long term, European co-operation to abolish restrictions and all other discriminatory practices. Two men, Jean Monnet and Robert Schuman, strove to bring about European cooperation. Their hope was that this would finally put an end to Franco-German rivalry by forging economic links between these two countries and the rest of Europe, thus making a rupture impossible. The European union they conceived of was to create a vast common market of capital, workers and merchandise, comparable to that of the United States, whose productivity growth and general prosperity had benefited from the abolition of customs barriers.

This organization was constructed in stages, not without objections – on the one hand, from protectionists and nationalists anxious to retain national independence, and on the other from the parties of the far Left. The latter campaigned against west European unity not only because they were inclined to see in it a war machine directed against the USSR and the People's Democracies, but also because the principal apostles of cooperation were, at the time, the heads of conservative parties, Christian Democrats who held power in various

39 Signing of the Treaty of Rome, 25 March 1957

western European countries: Alcide de Gasperi of Italy; Robert Schuman of France; Konrad Adenauer, the chancellor of West Germany. The leftists denounced the formation of this 'Vatican Europe' as a shock-army in the service of the United States.

We have already noted the first stages (p. 26), which were the formation of the Organization for European Economic Cooperation in 1948, and then of the European Payments Union in 1950. This was followed up by an integration and expansion of markets in a limited and technical centre, the European Coal and Steel Community (1952), which was intended to balance the production and sale of coal and steel by six countries: West Germany, France, Italy and the three members of Benelux – Belgium, Luxembourg and the Netherlands. In 1949 localized customs union projects had been outlined, e.g. Nordek, to include the Scandinavian countries, and one between France and Italy, but these came to nothing. On the other hand, Benelux was successful in developing trade without, however, going as far towards economic integration as had been hoped for at the time of its formation in 1953.

61

In 1955 the question was raised of a union of the Six for joint research in atomic energy (Euratom was finally realized in 1957) and the creation of an economic community through reduction of customs duties. In 1957 a treaty was signed in Rome which foresaw a transitional period during which restrictive practices and internal customs duties would be progressively reduced and ultimately disappear, leaving only a common external tariff. The object clearly defined by Paul H. Spaak was 'to lead the states in a kind of irreversible economic and political process without the risk of setting conditions which any one of the states might find intolerable'. Since then, the application of this formula has been pursued and expanded, thanks to the decisions of the conference at The Hague in December 1969.

The Agricultural Charter of the Common Market adopted at Rome led to the progressive unification of wheat prices, not without some extremely lively struggles, from 1962 to 1967. An agreement was also reached on the free circulation of goods, services, capital and people. The right to set up businesses throughout the Community was also established, after legislation relating to banks and the liberal professions had been coordinated; it included mutual recognition of professional certificates, but excluded grave risk to the labour market and restrictions necessitated by considerations of public order and health. In 1965 a provisional agreement was made with a view towards a common transport policy through the elimination of discriminatory tariff measures. But the return of monetary instability (devaluation of the franc and revaluation of the 'floating' DM in 1969, plus the unfavourable effects this had in both countries) has once again put in question the functioning of the common agricultural market which was agreed with so much difficulty in Brussels in 1967. Finally, the conference at The Hague decided that the common agricultural policy should come into force in 1975.

This was the groundwork, already well advanced, for the unification of a vast market of 170,000,000 consumers within the frame of a common economic policy, which is intended ultimately to equalize competition (through prohibition of private agreements, monopolies and government subsidies except for the purpose of helping underdeveloped regions). What remains is to unify the economic policies of the EEC members, to equalize living and working conditions through unification of employment legislation, social security, protection against accidents, and union law – and above all to create monetary unity, which the events of 1969 showed to be indispensable.

A European investment bank has been created to facilitate improvement of underdeveloped areas, modernization of plant and the fulfilment of projects undertaken by several states jointly.

In 1961 Greece obtained the special status of associate member of the EEC; the Six undertake to buy a third of its exports. Turkey, which had requested the same privileges, entered into negotiations which have not yet been concluded.

Sceptical for a long time of the Common Market's chances of success, Great Britain refused to join. Then, when it saw a protected west European zone being formed, it began in 1959 to construct a European Free Trade Association (EFTA), unifying seven European countries: Great Britain, the three Scandinavian countries, Switzerland, Austria and Portugal. In 1961 and 1962 these countries of the 'small zone of free trade' applied for admission to EEC, but the conditions laid down by Great Britain (preservation of its traditional links with the Commonwealth, protection of British agriculture because of its peculiar situation, maintenance of its privileged relations with the other EFTA countries) were met, after prolonged negotiations in Brussels, with a brutal veto by General de Gaulle (14 January 1963). Great Britain, he said, was 'held back by the weight of its empire'. Since that time, the majority of British opinion seems to have rallied towards entry into the Common Market (though most recently there have been signs of uncertainty), and this is hoped for by all who believe that Europe, deprived of British participation, will remain crippled in spite of the undeniable prosperity achieved by EEC.

Finally, in 1961, eighteen new African republics and French-speaking Malagasy began negotiations with a view towards association in the Common Market. The Africans objected to the ill-concealed colonialism behind the proposal to create a Euroafrica, with its ill-conceived idea of preserving – under colour of preferential tariffs and financial assistance – the old colonial regime: Africa furnishing raw materials and buying manufactured products from Europe. On the other hand, there was a sharp struggle among the European states whose interests differed strongly according to whether they had been colonial powers (France and Belgium) or had never, or no longer, had African colonies (Germany and the Netherlands). Finally, in 1962 a convention of association was signed for five years and a European development fund was created to finance works of land- and production-development.

In 1964 Israel was also accorded special relations with the EEC, following a commercial agreement. Austria, the major part of whose trade is with the Six, came up against Italy's opposition because of incidents in South Tyrol; Switzerland (because of its neutrality), Denmark, Norway and Sweden have also been kept out. As for the Irish Republic, its request for membership in January 1962 was rejected through pressure from the northern counties (Ulster) and the British government.

The results for the Six have unquestionably been beneficial. The most protectionist groups (particularly agriculture, which has had to transform itself) and wage-earners who feared unemployment, have come to see the advantages of the Common Market. Businesses are in the process of concentrating and integrating; all have sought to modernize, in order to be in a position to offer competitive prices, by reducing their overheads and winning new outlets, and by co-ordinating their efforts to overcome the serious technological backwardness of Europe. P. Drouin calls this 'a "cumulative process" of growth, in so far as the greater the scale of production, the easier it is to obtain loans'.

Comecon
In the face of a Europe of the Six whose economy is dominated by that of the United States, the eastern bloc organized itself more slowly and in a much less extreme way. After the reinforcement of its political and ideological bonds through the formation of Cominform, which coordinates the activities of the Communist Parties, the Moscow-based Comecon (Council of Mutual Economic Assistance) was created in January 1949. Up to 1948, the eastern economies had developed national plans in an autarchic spirit, building up unprofitable and sometimes competitive industries in an irrational way and without coordination; at the same time, they still retained the three economic sectors: private, nationalized and cooperative. After 1948 they began to reconstruct themselves on the Soviet model, giving priority to the development of heavy industries and armaments. Yugoslavia has remained apart despite the reconciliation of 1956 with the eastern bloc.

Comecon is not a system of integration, submitting production to a supranational authority like the European Coal and Steel Community, but simply a centre for the coordination of plans and cooperation on the technical, scientific and financial levels. Within this group, with such varied and abundant but ill-distributed resources, great efforts were made after 1962 to organize the productivity of each national economy by the rational introduction of industries in such a way as to avoid redundancy as well as the waste of raw materials, time, fuel and transport. A council which meets once a year orients general policy, and an executive committee, composed of the vice-presidents of member states' Councils of Ministers, prepares the distribution of work and controls its fulfilment with the help of a Bureau, a Secretariat and eighteen permanent specialized commissions by sector (e.g. Intermetall coordinates the production of the machine industries of the six states). Each country remains master of its own plans; the unanimous decisions taken by the council are simply suggestions transmitted to the individual countries. The group has taken shape slowly: the International Bank of Economic Cooperation dates from 1964, and it was only in 1966 that the prices of the Comecon countries were aligned with world prices in order to facilitate trade with the west.

Since the rupture between east and west, the patterns of trade, which had been preserved until then, had to be broken and a new orientation imposed; this was all the more difficult as trade was struck by a series of prohibitions aimed at 'strategic' materials. The trade of the People's Democracies among themselves and with the USSR rose from 7 to 70 and 80 per cent. At the beginning there were short-term bilateral agreements; then, after 1950, as the five-year plans came into effect, long-term agreements appeared, marked by a more or less total renunciation of autarchy, the transformation of industrial structures, and more advanced technical cooperation. In 1954 the coordination of production plans through multilateral cooperation was organized with a view to creating large combines, capable of producing profitable ranges of goods; it was also intended to originate new distribution patterns and a rational division of labour among complementary countries. The effects appeared during the period 1960–65: joint investment agreements between Rumania and Yugoslavia, between East Germany and Poland (employment of Polish coal and unification of the power network from the Ukraine's high-tension grid with the distribution point at Prague), and between Poland, Czechoslovakia and East Germany. Specialization operates in certain service industries: East Germany and Poland undertake maritime transport and shipbuilding; Poland, Czechoslovakia and Hungary concentrate on aeroplane construction; Czechoslovakia and East

65

Germany cooperate in the construction of railroad trucks with interchangeable axles and an international railroad depot. Air transport regulations have been made uniform; Danubian navigation has been improved by the deepening of the river above and below Vienna at the same time as dams have been constructed for hydroelectric power; the 'Friendship' pipeline has been built for the oil from Baku which arrives at Schwedt on the Oder. The same specialization governs the use of raw materials and power, as well as capital investment: Poland, the Balkan countries and Hungary furnish agricultural products to Czechoslovakia, East Germany and, in part, the USSR; Hungary does not construct blast-furnaces, but provides bauxite, optical instruments (like East Germany), telecommunications equipment, etc.

Since 1960, international relaxation has favoured the development of relations between the east and the 'third-world' countries. International payments have been facilitated by the International Bank of Economic Cooperation; its capital of 300,000,000 transferable roubles enables it to play the role of a clearing bank, to finance investments among member states, and to regulate transactions with states that are not members. Thus trade with the latter has made progress, as well as with the United States and the countries of western Europe. This applies also to the underdeveloped countries, anxious not to be dependent exclusively on the United States – principally India, the United Arab Republic, Indonesia, Cuba and, up to 1960, China. The USSR and Czechoslovakia offer credits on advantageous terms to the 'third-world' countries.

POLITICAL AND TRADE-UNION FORCES

Ever since the nineteenth century when, under the system of *laisser-faire*, the Industrial Revolution created a downtrodden working class, prohibited by legislation from uniting to improve its conditions, Socialist theoreticians have been proposing solutions to the social problem. More or less clandestine organizations were founded under various forms to exert pressure against both employers and government.

The formation of trade unions; their legal recognition in Great Britain, paralleled by political movements which won extension of the vote to a large part, if not the whole, of the working class; the founding of Socialist Parties which became increasingly powerful – these events forced the different states, willingly or not, to entertain social reforms and, more and more, to take trade-union power into account. But the subsequent division of the Socialists into rival sects served to weaken their influence. Nevertheless, with varying speed, the Socialist Parties increased the number of their adherents, along with the rise of trade unions. The Socialist International was reconstituted in 1889 on the basis of Marxist doctrine and the class struggle, but the national parties were weak and – despite apparent unity – divided on numerous questions and tactics.

These divisions, which begot many and frequent splits, explain the failure of the International and the Socialist Parties when the threat of war became evident in 1914, and their inability to prevent the catastrophe. Then the Soviet Revolution quickly provoked within the Socialist Parties and the trade-union organizations a deep schism between those who remained in favour of revolution by force and those who called themselves 'reformist'. In addition, Fascism, in control of part of Europe in 1939, and then the occupation by the Nazi army, soon reduced the workers' movements to impotence and underground activities.

After 1945, political parties revived, and the trade-union movement made great strides. The trend towards reformism has been marked; the reconstruction of the Socialist International has resulted only in bringing together the parties of the NATO or affiliated countries, or friends of the International Confederation of Free Trade Unions (ICFTU), in which American trade unions exercise considerable influence through the size of their contribution, their anti-Communist orientation and policies in favour of class cooperation. The British Labour Party and the Swedish trade unionists seek nothing more than the improvement of the working class's standard of living, and the maintenance of full employment and the stability of prices. In spite of lip-service to Marxism, reformism has removed it from the Socialist spectrum. General prosperity, full employment, the disappearance of serious economic crises have weakened social antagonism – except in France and Italy, where powerful Communist Parties still exist, solidly implanted in the working class. Since the fear of Communism has been reinforced by the Czech *coup d'état* and the military occupation of Czechoslovakia in 1968, the transformation of the capitalist economic structure is no longer envisaged except by legal means. This moderate policy was always that of the British Labour Party (the first to produce a Welfare State plan), and also of the Scandinavian countries, among which Sweden, with its policy of general welfare, a system of complete social insurance and a strongly progressive income tax, seems to be the model.

In Great Britain, the number of trade-union members, which was over 6,000,000 in 1938, reached the considerable total of 9,800,000 in 1960. The Labour Party's accession to power in 1945 permitted the carrying out of their nationalization programme and the repeal of restrictive labour legislation passed by the Conservatives in 1927. Labour also imposed higher income tax and death duties. But economic difficulties caused by the crisis in international trade forced them, in 1948, to adopt stabilization of wages and prices, though with little effect, and to devalue the pound. Since acceptance of the Marshall Plan, British trade unionism has been powerfully influenced by the example of the combined American Federation of Labor and Congress of Industrial Organization (AFL/CIO), which refuses any joint action with the Communists, and favours methods less and less hostile to collaboration with the government, whichever party may be in power. The British trade unions thus tend increasingly to play a limited technical role. In 1951 the Labour Party and the trade unions, apparently having exhausted their programme, lost the General Election. Nevertheless, the General Council of the Trades Union Congress agreed to participate in a national commission created by the Conservatives to focus on a plan for economic expansion, and was authorized to formulate a general wages policy. In this way the integration of the trade unions into the capitalist system was reinforced.

The German trade-union movement, underground since 1933, was quickly reconstructed after the war. In 1949 the Confederation of German Trade Unions (DGB) was formed in the west by the union of the sixteen industrial unions (IG); from nearly 5,000,000 members in 1949, it grew to 6,574,000 in 1954. The proportion in relation to the total number of workers has remained constant at about 28·8 per cent since 1963. There are now many members of the DGB in the Bundestag, and the organization plays an important role in the development of social legislation; it also takes part in the self-management of social security organization, with the right to examine sickness-benefit accounts. It adopted many concepts of North American trade unionism, omitting from its statutes any reference to Marxism and rallying openly to the new capitalism. Besides the DGB, which exercises a virtual monopoly, there exist the Christian Federation of Workers (CGB) with 240,000 members, the

40 A political discussion:
painting by Guttuso (1959–60)

41 'The boss needs you
– you don't need him':
Paris left-wing poster, May 1968

Union of German Employees (DAG) with 500,000 members, and a Confederation of German Civil Servants with 707,000. Within the DGB there is a Right and a Left; this forces the organization to maintain a very moderate stand and to follow an orientation related to no particular ideology. The Godesberg programme adopted by the Social Democratic Party in 1959 condemned Communism because 'the change in the ownership of property has caused the disappearance of liberty' and because 'the dictatorship of the proletariat is no longer a reality in our time'. Instead, it demanded an increasingly extensive democratization of political and economic life. It does not demand collective appropriation of the means of production, but the scaling of wages to the cost of living, equality with the employer in decisions (*Mitbestimmung*) and a voice in management. The DGB's preponderance is a result of its mass organization; it is, in fact, the only representative spokesman, as far as the employers are concerned, in co-management. It has become a powerful pressure group. Thanks to its members' contributions, it is a real financial power, running more than 120 trade-union centres, as well as schools, youth clubs, banks, insurance companies; it participates in numerous enterprises of all types, publishes newspapers and controls news agencies.

As for the German Social Democratic Party, it has established itself in the new capitalist society and follows the path of participation by calling for an 'improved capitalism'; it no longer has to worry about being outbid on its Left by the Communist Party, which was outlawed in West Germany in 1956, and has been allowed since 1969 in a different and curtailed form. Of all the Socialist Parties of western Europe it is the most anti-Communist and has virtually adopted the Christian Socialist programme. According to the Godesberg programme it is 'the party of the liberty of the spirit', it accepts 'the free collaboration of the churches' and assures them the protection of civil law, it affirms its total loyalty to the constitution, renounces nationalization, and admits 'free competition and free initiative for the entrepreneur'. The party of the workers has become 'the party of the people'. This moderation no doubt explains its electoral success in October 1969 and the formation, for the first time since 1930, of a government presided over by a Social Democratic chancellor.

In France the situation is more complex. Here the decline of the Socialist Party is complete. With 354,000 members in 1946, and only 100,000 in 1960, its 'humanist socialism', defined by Léon Blum in a fundamentally anti-Communist book (*A l'échelle humaine*), proposes to free man via the route of democratic socialism. In parliament it practised a policy of alliance with the Right Centre, the aim of which was the creation of an intermediary 'third force' between the Communist Left and the Gaullist party, a negative policy which turned the Socialists into 'hostages of the Left in cabinets of the Right Centre', and prevented them from effecting any important social reform. In fact the party even renounced its defence of lay public schools; for a long time it supported the policy of repression against the emancipation movements in the Asian colonies and Africa; it undertook a preventive war against Egypt in 1956. In 1969 it adopted a position even more hostile to an understanding with the Communist Party, making itself in consequence more powerless than ever.

The trade-union movement in France is simply crumbling, to the point where each of the three rival groups refuses to make known the number of its members. The strongest working-class elements have remained faithful to the General Confederation of Labour (CGT) which is under the control of the Communist Party. The former French Confederation of Christian Workers (CFTC), which expanded with the increase of white-collar workers, split into two groups in 1964; one abandoned the 'Christian' label in hopes of attracting the non-clerical moderate element, and is now the French Democratic Confederation of Labour (CFDT), the other, much smaller, is the old 'CFTC preserved'. Finally, in a third split following those of 1921 and 1939, the Workers' Force (FO) separated from the CGT in 1947 in an anti-Communist gesture and assembled, under the influence of the Socialist Party, those anti-Communist employees who later refused to join the CFDT (1964) because of its confessional origins. Another organization is the National Educational Federation (FEN), comprising a large majority of professors and schoolmasters; there are also the railway-workers' union and the postal-workers' union, both of which are split into various factions; and the General Confederation of Executives (CGC), which consists of engineers, technicians and certain civil servants.

Labour agitation has only spasmodically been important in France, arising particularly on the subject of employment (the issue being reduction of working-hours) and in the crisis sectors: the shipyards of Brittany, the coal mines in the north, centre and the Cévennes region. For the same reasons, farmers have been involved in acts of violence and conflicts with the police when expressing their demands. In the public and quasi-public sectors, labour demonstrations are

71

42 Overproduction leads French farmers to dump surplus tomatoes

most often a matter of one-day strikes in support of claims, while major strikes of long duration have been rare: the miners and railway-workers in 1947, another general miners' strike in October 1948 in which troops intervened with violence, another in the summer of 1953, one in 1963 when the miners ignored a requisition, and finally the general strike in June 1968 which involved 9,000,000 workers in all three sectors – private, public and nationalized. Nevertheless, the divisions in the French trade-union movement have never been so great.

In Italy, the Socialist Party split in January 1947, as a result of tendencies towards participation and moderation in its right wing (which became the Italian Social Democratic party under Giuseppe Saragat). In 1948, the bulk of the party, under the direction of Pietro Nenni and Lelio Basso, formed a Common Front with the Communists. This resulted in a very active group of the extreme Left, which was, however, a minority in face of the powerful majority of the Christian Democrats. The impossibility of making an impression on the bloc in power and obtaining necessary reforms (such as the repeal of a great deal of Fascist legislation which remains in force) led Nenni, in 1957, to seek an alliance with the left wing of the Christian Democrats, who also wished to achieve certain reforms. This move, from the Christian Democrat point of view, was called the 'opening to the Left', but the experiment proved disappointing and no reforms, except for the nationalization of electrical power, resulted from it. The consequent immobility caused several splits which further weakened the influence of the Socialists.

The divisions of the workers among themselves and the division between rival organizations are the principal reason for the weakness of the wage-earning class. Nor is there any sign of healing these divisions, for the categories of workers are becoming more diverse and numerous as technological progress continues. This results in salary differentials which lead those in the higher categories to distinguish themselves from the rest, and even to create particular unions which sometimes refuse to participate in the activities of the particular branch of work to which they belong.

Moreover, the division between rival organizations can be explained not only by Communism but by another ideological factor: the rejection or acceptance of the class struggle. On the one side there are organizations which, in the words of Marcel David, 'are ready to collaborate with a bourgeoisie still determined neither to relinquish the reins of power nor to sacrifice its interests'; on the other side, there are less conciliatory organizations which the government and employers view with hostility. It is easy for the latter to exploit the divisions between these groups and the personal rivalries of their leaders. In fact, divided and competing, the unions are definitely in a position of inferiority: unity of action is rarely achieved, and only for limited objectives. Hence it would be a mistake to believe that they can be an effective counterweight to the alliance of government and large interests, in spite of their claim to have learnt wisdom.

If the Socialist Parties, as well as the trade unions under their influence, have developed in this way, it is worth noting that the Communist Parties, too, do not occupy the same position they did in the past. While using revolutionary terminology and preparing for the complete transformation of social structure, the Communist Parties in those countries where they play an important role – notably Italy and France – have some notion nowadays of participating in government within a Left majority; thus they have been led to adopt more flexible tactics and a more realistic policy. The hypothesis of a violent revolution being barred, the only legal way to obtain power that remains open to them requires an electoral alliance with the Socialist or democratic parties of the middle classes, whose programmes are limited to the improvement of working conditions and social advance. Since they are a minority in spite of their progress and their solid roots among the workers, they have to accept the ground rules of parliamentary democracy by disavowing and fighting the 'Leftists', as they did in France in May-June 1968, when they refused all joint action with the Trotskyite, Marxist-Leninist, Maoist 'groups', and even with the hotheads of the CFDT, thus preventing the demonstrations and unrest from turning into bloody insurrection.

One may therefore conclude that, in the last twenty years, the social situation in western Europe has greatly changed. The evolution towards peacefulness, which began during the period between the two World Wars, has been accentuated: wildcat strikes have become the exception, official strikes have been less frequent and in general have ended quickly. Parties and organizations which were formerly revolutionary are gradually being integrated into the new capitalism.

LAND DEVELOPMENT AND HOUSING

A domain in which the state has had to intervene, to the extent of orienting private enterprise towards the improvement of living conditions, is the development of land and housing. The solutions applied have sometimes been so wide-ranging that they have completely altered the appearance of certain regions. The problem arises in all countries as a result of the rural exodus; but it has also been caused by the considerable displacements of population which occurred, first, immediately after the Second World War, and then with the return of nationals to the home country following the emancipation of colonies: Dutch and Eurasians, Belgians from the Congo, the French from Indo-China and Algeria, British colonists from India, South-East Asia and Africa. There has also been an immigration of foreign manual workers from distant and often poverty-stricken lands. Other factors were the widespread destruction caused by both aerial bombardment and military operations, and the lack of new construction or upkeep of housing (often already outdated) during the war. Here again, faced with a task beyond the capabilities of private enterprise, government has frequently had to take over.

But this question is linked with a much vaster problem, the development of land resources, i.e. the organizing of the various parts of the country as a function of the general interest as well as their own best use. An examination of the geographic distribution of the European peoples and their activities – industrial as well as agricultural – shows that there is an economically developed Europe which corresponds roughly to ancient Lotharingia: from the North Sea to the Mediterranean, it encompasses the Netherlands, the German Rhineland, Belgium, the north-east and south-east of France with Switzerland and northern Italy. This area contrasts strikingly with the regions bordering it on the east and west, where modern economic activity constitutes only small isolated islands in the midst of purely rural and poorly developed zones. Thus there is a general disequilibrium between the countries of Europe, and also between different regions of the same country. A less unequal and more rational arrangement of activities is necessary. This requires a better distribution of people, a geographical mobility which enables them to shift from overpopulated regions, with declining industries and unemployment, to those where new and growing activities create a demand for labour. It also entails a policy for the retraining of wage-earners whose jobs disappear with the closing or transfer of factories. The problem has arisen everywhere, but most acutely in Great Britain, France, Italy, Spain, Germany, Scandinavia, Poland and the USSR. In all countries it involves industrial decentralization and the creation of more harmonious and pleasant frameworks for living.

Town-planning has produced the best results in Great Britain and the Netherlands, both of them overpopulated and strongly urbanized, and in the Scandinavian countries where, on the contrary, labour is scarce and expensive but ill-distributed and where cities are constantly growing. Le Corbusier (whose *Cité radieuse* dates from 1935) and the Athens Charter of 1943 formulated the ideal conditions for improving regions and cities, as well as the criteria for all modern dwellings: creation of 'neighbourhood communities . . . each having autonomy and its own appearance', separated from neighbouring factories, with a maximum of 240 inhabitants per hectare; preservation of extensive space for public and private enterprises; decongestion of the centre of agglomeration by removing to the periphery all activities not essential to the centre. It was not a matter of creating new suburbs like those that exist around all large cities, constructed without plan according to the whim or resources of landowners, but rather of building harmonious, functional and integrated unities.

Great Britain has undertaken the most ambitious task by far:

75

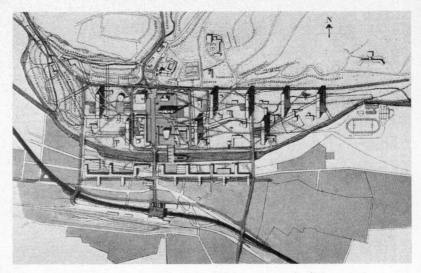

43 Le Corbusier's project for Saint-Dié, which was never built (see p. 86)

44 Cumbernauld new town, Scotland
45 Housing development at Roehampton near London ▶

complete remodelling of the country. There, the urgent need for constructing dwellings in considerable numbers, the existence of pockets of chronic unemployment, and a variety of economic problems, resulted in the passage of a number of laws, first drafted in 1943 and culminating in the Town and Country Planning Act of 1962. These laws set out the conditions for the construction and planning of new cities, as well as the development of smaller nuclei intended to bring about simultaneously the decongestion of large conurbations and the reorganization of their centre. Measures were taken to avoid speculation in land and construction, and fourteen new towns were distributed in a circle around London (among them Harlow, Stevenage, Hemel Hempstead, Bracknell, Crawley, Basildon and Welwyn), others in the Durham coal fields, in Wales and at Clydeside near Glasgow. Certain municipalities also made agreements with neighbouring cities for the construction of housing where overspill will live. London, for example, anticipates the 'export' of 1,000,000 Londoners before 1982.

At the same time certain regions have been redeveloped: new machine industries, special steelworks, plants for the manufacture of motor parts, electrical and electronic machinery, radios and automobiles are replacing shipyards, textile factories, metallurgical industries and coal mines in decline.

In Switzerland the policy of concentrating major industries is being pursued parallel with decentralization; this will stabilize the rural population and create medium-sized handicraft enterprises outside the large concentration zones of Zurich, Basle and Geneva. In Sweden, satellite cities (such as Vällingby) form a greater Stockholm of over 1,000,000 inhabitants around the capital. In Finland the garden-city Tapiola 9 km. from Helsinki, in Germany satellite towns near Bremen, Hamburg, Karlsruhe, Bielefeld and Berlin, serve to relieve the congestion within these built-up areas. At Trondheim and Bergen in the north of Norway, as in the conurbation of Oslo, efforts have been made to convert fishermen into farmers and industrial workers, particularly in the key industries which produce exports and benefit from large investments.

In France, regional disparities are also extremely serious. Of the ninety départements in existence before 1966, thirty-five had a density of less than 50 inhabitants per sq. km., while almost 55 per

46 High-rise housing in a suburb of Munich

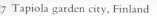

7 Tapiola garden city, Finland

48 Central precinct in Vällingby, Stockholm

49 Halen
near Berne

79

cent of the territory (Midi, centre, east, southern Alps, Corsica) contained only 32 per cent of the population. On the other hand, the Paris region comprised 8,500,000 inhabitants on 2·2 per cent of the country's territory, 15·8 per cent of the total population and 27 per cent of the urban population. Such were the features of the 'French desert' outside the crowded Paris agglomeration. If one adds that 48·7 per cent of industrial employment is at present located in eastern France, only 26·6 per cent in the western regions, and 24·7 per cent in the Paris area itself, one realizes the extent of this imbalance.

In order to reduce congestion in the Paris area, there have been attempts to build up industrial, commercial and administrative structures in the provinces by decentralization and developing medium-sized towns through the introduction of new factories and offices. There has also been an effort to avoid speculation in the rare green areas that surround the capital. With this double aim, it was decided to create on two axes – north (Pontoise-Meaux) and south (Meaux-Melun-Nantes) – eight distinct cities, linked to one another and to Paris by a strong transportation system; and, in addition, to assign priority development to nine more distant centres: Rouen, Le Havre, Le Mans, Caen, Tours, Orléans, Troyes, Rheims and Amiens. There is also a plan for developing seventeen important cities in the Rhône and Garonne valleys, and in the north-east and west, nine of which will be metropolitan areas intended to balance Paris. Certain branches of industry, which are in an irreversible state of decline (coal and iron mines in Pas-de-Calais and Lorraine), have to be converted. Mixed economies have been established to develop particular regions (Bas-Rhône-Languedoc, the Languedoc-Roussillon coast, the coast of Aquitaine, Corsica).

The drive for industrial decentralization has had only meagre results so far. The creation here and there of some thousands of employment opportunities has not prevented the population of the Paris agglomeration from continuing to grow, nor the depopulation of the countryside from becoming more marked at every level – even in favour of the market towns and local capitals.

Italy undertook the task of remodelling the country by working out certain reforms, principally to aid agriculture but also industry. The *Cassa per il Mezzogiorno* (Fund for the South) was instituted to divide up the large estates in western Sicily (in the region of Trapani, eight estates with 37,000 hectares have been distributed among 9,000 farmers), to build houses, carry out irrigation projects and re-affores-

50, 51 Industrialization in southern Italy. Above, computer centre in the Monteshell petro-chemical factory at Brindisi; below, fully automatic piercer at work in a Sicilian potash mine

tation, improve the infrastructure of roads and electrification, and to undertake drainage in the areas of Foggia, the plain of Silè and that of Gela. It provides subsidies and loans to industry; and ENI as well as IRI have had to invest 40 to 60 per cent of their capital in the south. Thirty-nine points of growth (twelve major and twenty-seven minor ones) were chosen for a concentration of effort, the state offering fiscal advantages and other customary stimulations: credits, reduced transportation tariffs, etc. In this way the development of the growth-points of Gela (petrochemicals), Bagnoli near Naples, Cagliari, Bari, Brindisi, Taranti and Ragusa was initiated.

In Spain the regional development plan of 1964–67 was much tardier. It aims at reducing the disparities among the group of twelve provinces containing 47 per cent of the population and 57·7 per cent of total production, and those which, with 42·2 per cent of the country's territory, contain only 20·6 per cent of the population and 15·25 per cent of production. To this end, there is a project for the creation of industrial points of growth (Corunna, Seville, Valladolid, Vigo, Saragossa, Huelva, Burgos), five of which are situated outside the most immediately profitable sectors. One of the poorest areas of Spain has benefited since 1953 from a 'plan of colonization, industrialization and electrification', called the 'Badajoz plan', the results of which – though the work is still in progress – show a clear growth in productivity and a doubling of family expenditures. It constitutes a success in a region which is unfortunately narrowly localized.

NEW TOWN-PLANNING

This aspect of the political economy of states that suffer from imbalance among regions, and between city and country, must not make us lose sight of the fact that urbanization has changed the patterns of town-planning. There have been moves to alter the construction of industrial complexes and those for collective use so as to make life more pleasant in the factory or community. For example, around the factories of Flins in France there are gardens, a stadium, theatres, meeting-halls, sports areas, as well as housing for the employees. Nowadays many factories look like administration buildings. This is true of new hospitals and schools, which are clean, neat, and have a unified appearance: buildings harmoniously distributed around a green space and integrated as an ensemble. Classrooms and hospital accommodations are oriented towards light and sun, with ample facilities for ventilation. Such efforts can be seen in the University of Bordeaux, the open-air school of Bruderholz near Basle, schools in Hertfordshire, the Rheims lycée, the Saint-Antoine hospital centre in Paris, and the cantonal hospital in Zurich. A dual artistic and functional character is evident in the railway-stations of Rome and Florence, in many European airports, in the Rome sports stadium designed by Nervi, in the museum at Le Havre and the UNESCO building in Paris. The elegant success of the Lijnbann in Rotterdam, a commercial street of 650 yds. reserved exclusively for pedestrians, is also noteworthy.

The joint work of architects and engineers has often had happy results, primarily in the abandonment of slow and expensive hand-production methods in favour of much more efficient techniques: the industrialization of building (which Le Corbusier called for as long ago as 1925), standardization and prefabrication in large units. There has been success in overcoming the prejudice against sky-scrapers, which are the least costly formula for construction and maintenance, and which are inevitable in view of the excessive price of land and the shortage of free space.

With the exception of such countries as Finland, Sweden and Great Britain, whose governments have taken in hand the implementation of large-scale plans and have imposed regulations on developers, reconstruction left to private initiative has not always had happy results. It is only when the state or local authorities provide subsidies, or where building cooperatives exist, as in Belgium, the Netherlands and West Germany, that the rate of building is satisfactory and the laws of profitability are not brought into play.

Speculation in land and construction, and the usurious rates of loans from banks and other credit institutions have created a situation in which low-priced family dwellings and medium-rental housing are beyond the workers' means. It was not until 1953 that France achieved 100,000 new dwellings; in 1960 the figure was 360,000. In West Germany by that year 551,000 dwellings had been built, in Great Britain 304,000. These figures were far outstripped by the USSR, where the proportion of dwellings per 1,000 inhabitants is the highest, West Germany and the Scandinavian countries coming next. Forty-three per cent of dwellings in Finland and 41 per cent in Norway were built between 1945 and 1965, but in Finland there are still 27 per cent of dwellings with two people per room.

52 UNESCO building, Paris

53 Vickers Tower, London

55 Shopping centre (Hötorget) in Stockholm

56 *Métro Station Opéra*, painting by Willem Van Genk (1964)

◀ 54 Nervi's sports arena in Rome

The desire to create clearly individualized groups of dwellings, to preserve the largest possible area of green space, and to facilitate traffic (the ideal would be to create roads with differentiated functions) has inspired certain architects and engineers to happy inventions, some of them extremely successful. This is the case in Coventry, destroyed in the blitz of 1941: here pedestrian and motor traffic has been completely separated. This has been achieved also in Stevenage, where the centre (the 'precinct') is prohibited to automobiles.

Although the family house retains its partisans in Great Britain, it has not been possible to do without high-rise buildings: the Hilton Hotel in London is over 320 ft. tall, the Post Office tower over 600 ft. tall, Vickers Tower some 380 ft. For lack of space, some British local authorities, including new towns such as Cumbernauld, have had to build housing estates of 10-storey buildings. Nevertheless, towns and whole neighbourhoods have been built with all the new requirements in mind. But the most common formula in all suburbs, and in the heart of medium-sized towns, is that of large groups characterized by the alternation of 4-storey apartment-blocks without lifts and apartment towers of 15 storeys or more. In order to avoid monotony, the colours of doors and windows are varied. (In Hemel Hempstead there are 100 different types of houses, in Crawley 250.) At the same time the frontage is varied so as to procure the greatest possible exposure to sunshine and light; large buildings are often planned in broken or curved lines.

These constructions are models for all other countries of Europe, which adapt them to their own landscape and climate, while respecting national traditions: the use of wood and brick in Denmark, for example, and the Swedish preference for coloured materials. Le Corbusier drew up a very novel project for the reconstruction of Saint Dié, but unfortunately it was abandoned. All he has left us are the 'unités d'habitation' of Marseilles and Nantes-Rezé, which are vertical cities, but deprived of their natural framework. He realized his views fully only in Chandigarh, India. Nevertheless, the reconstruction of the old town of Mulhouse by Lurçat, of Sotteville-les-Rouen and Royan, the 'cité Paul Langevin' at Saint-Denis, the towns of Mourenx near Lacq, Toulouse-le-Mirail and Bagnols-sur-Cèze, and the renovation of the centre and basilica of Saint-Denis, are all examples of successful ventures in France.

The number of foreign workers and of peasants leaving the countryside is so great that it is impossible to house them in these new constructions. They crowd together in obsolete premises within the city, or outside the cities they create 'black villages', shanty-towns, *bidonvilles* in France, *borgate* in Italy, formed by agglomerations of cabins, huts, abandoned trucks, lacking in any plumbing or the most elementary sanitary conditions. Nevertheless, much has been accomplished and there have been many innovations which will ultimately improve general living conditions. A great deal remains to be done in the matter of housing, especially in the Mediterranean countries and France, so that every inhabitant may have a decent home; it is precisely in this area that efforts on behalf of those least blessed in life have been the most belated.

CO-MANAGEMENT, SELF-MANAGEMENT AND WORKERS' PARTICIPATION

'Man does not live by bread alone'; and for a long time, wage-earners have been claiming not only a more substantial share in the profits of their employers, but also a role in management – an 'industrial democracy', and an end to the 'autocracy of the managing director'.

On this point, employers' resistance has been particularly obdurate and in practice has not yet been effectively breached. Even though wage-earners in almost every field have, through widespread collective agreements, obtained important improvements in working conditions, pay, social services and guarantees against arbitrary dismissal, employers remain inflexible on what is called co-management. This refusal can be accounted for by the wish to keep control of the firm's policy and hierarchical structure, as well as the deeply rooted managerial idea of what was once called 'proprietorship by divine right': i.e. the employer, the proprietor, as the sole master of decisions, just as the naval commander is sole master 'after God' on board ship.

As Pierre Drouin puts it, 'There is a propensity on the part of certain employers to regard anything that questions the structures, and particularly the legitimacy, of power based on proprietorship as injurious to the firm's possibilities of expansion or its manœuvrability.' This is why the works committees established in France in 1946 have not developed; their activity has consisted essentially, if not exclusively, in the management of social works, without the right of inspecting financial administration, investments or general direction – without even any information on the state, good or bad, of business or on the firm's 'policy'. In small and medium-sized enterprises, the committees' activity is nil; sometimes they do not exist at all. The programme of the government formed by General de Gaulle's successor in 1969 calls for 'participation' and a 'continuous dialogue' between the workers' organizations on the one side, and the employers and the state on the other, but it remains to be seen whether this will have any practical effect.

Sweden and Denmark are the only states which have adopted a rule of publishing all private documentation in the press, just as the government does in the case of public and judicial matters; this assures the 'transparency of employers' power' and is limited only by 'problems whose divulgence might prejudice a firm's success'.

West Germany is the only country which introduced, in 1951 and 1952, workers' representatives into the boards of directors of businesses; in the mining and metal industries the supervisory boards consist of eleven representatives: five for the workers, five for the shareholders, and an eleventh neutral member, coopted by the other ten. This board elects the executive committee (*Vorstand*), which includes a director of labour, who cannot be named against the advice of the workers' representatives, and who is generally put up by the union. In the smaller firms there is a works council (*Betriebsrat*) elected directly by the personnel in secret ballot; it keeps watch over the observance of contractual agreements and can, within certain limits, block dismissals. A labour tribunal or a commission made up of equal representatives of labour and management decides in cases of conflict with the employer. Management is confided (where there are more than 100 employees) to an economic council of equal representation, on which the representatives of the personnel are designated by the works council.

In this way a method of collaboration has been established between employers and employees, facilitated by the existence of a single trade-union organization, the DGB, whose congress in 1965 demanded extension of the system to firms with more than 2,000 employees. The employers opposed this energetically out of fear that it would interfere with the speed of decision-making. Similar demands were also made by the Confederation of Christian Trade Unions in Belgium, the Valkhoff commission in the Netherlands, and the British Labour Party. In Britain co-determination in fact already exists in some of the nationalized industries, and there are opportunities for its extension through the Joint Consultative Committees, on which representatives of labour are required.

As for self-management, we encounter it in France in nationalized industries in the form of a committee which represents the interests of workers, employees, consumers and the state. Outside of this, there is hardly an example of self-management in France except for the production cooperatives which exist, in small number, only in the building trades; these seem to have no future, for they are less effectual than private firms.

Another solution is provided by the idea of a 'people's capitalism' which has appeared in West Germany and Austria as a result of the denationalization of large firms nationalized in 1945: for example, Volkswagen's capital is divided into registered shares of DM 50, which have been transferred at 20 per cent discount to workers earning less than DM 9,000 a year. In Austria the government retains 50 per cent of the capital of the two largest banks, the Credit Anstalt-Bankverein and the Österreichische Länderbank; the rest (800,000 shares) has been sold at 115 per cent of par value to small subscribers earning less than 7,000 Schillings per year at the first bank, and less than 4,000 at the second.

Some large French firms (e.g. the Péchiney aluminium works) have distributed non-transferable shares *gratis* to their employees, but these are cases of private initiatives which have not been widely imitated, though Imperial Chemical Industries has a similar scheme in England.

Except for these last forms of association, the reforms achieved often give personnel an opportunity to be less passive, but do not yet offer them an active role in management. Nevertheless, even these limited changes represent a beginning in the integration of the new capitalist society.

THE ADVENT OF MASS CULTURE
AND MEASURES OF SOCIAL APPEASEMENT

The Welfare State

In the front rank of 'lessons of the war' was the memory of the Great Depression and the distress of millions of unemployed or underemployed workers. This calamity was one of the principal reasons for the spread of Fascism and the great slaughter. It had, therefore, to be eliminated, and this was President Franklin D. Roosevelt's programme: to combat unemployment, poverty, sickness and war. The Beveridge Plan of 1944 in Great Britain provided the example. Fear of revolution and a desire for social appeasement stimulated the governments of western Europe to action in 1945. Thus it may not be too much to say that, since the end of the war, all governments in the west have been sensitive to these problems and have set themselves the aim of creating and expanding a prosperity which would benefit all classes. This preoccupation dominates the political history of Europe since 1945.

Pressures from the people and electoral considerations have forced governments to act in such a way as to ensure the continued growth of prosperity and a more equal distribution of 'the slices of the cake' than before. At present an annual salary growth rate of 3 to 4 per cent is considered an indispensable minimum. Everywhere people aspire to rise in the social scale, and to secure access to occupations with higher pay as well as enhanced social status. The response has not been equal, but it is general: all governments have devoted an increasing portion of their budgets to social investments. In 1965 it varied between 14·2 and 15·1 per cent according to country. This desire for betterment has been strengthened by industrial growth and technological sophistication which demands an increased number of highly qualified technicians. Furthermore, over and above the cost of public services and armaments, the increased birth-rate and higher life-expectancy have burdened the working population with the expense of caring for children and old people; that is, public resources have to be augmented, and this can be done only through an increase in national revenue produced by a greater yield of taxation.

The two necessities of maintaining social peace and increasing the state's resources have thus contributed to an improvement in the standard of living. Since 1945 every European country has experienced higher wages, shorter working hours, paid holidays, full employment and the virtual disappearance of unemployment, construction of wholesome and cheap housing, social security protection against sickness, loss of work, and old age. As in the case of production, we must distinguish between eastern and western Europe because the point of departure and the setting up of new institutions in the former have given the social evolution characteristics which are noticeably different from those in the west.

Great Britain deserves credit for boldly opening the way by being the first to introduce a comprehensive social security system. The Report prepared by a committee presided over by Sir William Beveridge determined the guidelines for a system unlike any that had existed before. This Report considered social insurance as part of a coherent policy of social progress: at the same time a means of redistributing wealth, fighting sickness, ignorance and lack of hygiene, and

57, 58 Improved working conditions. Left, Austrian poster (1961) demanding early closing of shops on Saturday; right, French poster on the solidarity of social security

assuring the destitute of an income. Therefore it guarantees reimbursement for the expenses of illness, surgery and their sequels, assistance and paid maternity leave for young mothers, accident and infirmity insurance, old-age insurance which provides (at the age of 65 for men, 60 for women) for those no longer capable of active occupation.

The manner of applying such measures varies according to country: those that are most highly industrialized and enjoy the most advanced economic development have the most coherent and general social security systems. The former opposition of conservative parties has weakened and all countries have now been won over to the welfare state. They apply it with greater or less zeal and conviction, while its critics denounce it as a cause of waste and an encouragement to indolence. Nevertheless, the British plan and the laws it inspired have been imitated everywhere with varying generosity in its provisions.

In France before 1930, certain firms gave their personnel family allowances; these firms became less competitive as their overheads

91

increased in this way. A few years later, obligatory funds were set up, to which all employers contributed and the benefits were distributed among workers as a whole. Then, by the Family Code of 1939, employers' funds were required to pay a bonus for a worker's first child; and in 1946 these employers' funds were replaced by family allowance funds, managed jointly by employers and workers. This was an effort to encourage the having of children and to reduce the disadvantages of large families in relation to the childless. It was in 1945 that social security was organized in earnest to take the place of the old system of social insurance (1930). The different schemes which previously applied to various categories of the population were unified and in 1961 the system was extended to agricultural workers. Since 1966 its administration has been entrusted to a single fund.

Sweden has the most generous and complete social security system. It absorbs a third of the state's total expenditure and of local and provincial budgets, and represents more than one-sixth of the net national income. Here, too, contributions are paid by those who are insured, by the employers and by the state in variable proportions. In West Germany, Italy and France, a sum equal to about 30 per cent of wages is laid out on social security. These social taxes have considerably reduced the disparity between incomes, especially in Sweden.

Since the fear of unemployment is the main preoccupation of wage-earners and government, many measures have been adopted to ensure full employment. The requirements of reconstruction, the growth of population and economic expansion have made achievement of this goal much easier. Industrial unemployment has diminished, or even disappeared, except in some isolated, neglected or backward regions, such as exist in Belgium, Italy and certain parts of the British Isles. General prosperity has even made it necessary to use foreign labour, which has become so important that the expansion of certain industries is closely dependent on it. Immigrant workers provoke grave problems, even in Great Britain where a liberal attitude towards foreigners and the absence of racialism have been traditional. The arrival of coloured workers, even though they are British subjects from the Commonwealth, has become an extremely serious issue. These immigrants constitute a proletariat, often leading a wretched type of life. Agitation has encouraged racialism, which is vigorously fought by the authorities, but the trade unions most concerned, who fear the holding down of wages, demand that the state limit immigration and look on this growing racialism with some complacency. In Germany the number of workers from southern countries – Turks, Greeks, Spaniards, Portuguese, Yugoslavs, and even Jordanians – has reached 900,000 and they have become indispensable in spite of full employment. In Switzerland, where the number of foreign workers has multiplied eightfold in ten years and where they have comprised one-third of the labour force since 1956, the government began in 1960 to take measures to limit the number of annual arrivals. In France there has been a spate (sometimes clandestine) of Spaniards, Portuguese, North Africans, Senegalese and Mauritians; as in other countries they have the least well paid, most difficult and unhealthy jobs (mining and chemicals).

Even if the number of registered unemployed remains small and is officially less than 3 per cent, the situation is often much more serious because of underemployment in occupations whose productivity and remuneration are low or nil. In Great Britain in 1966, the unemployment figure exceeded 440,000 (1·9 per cent of wage-earners), after having reached nearly 900,000 in 1963 as a result of deflationary measures. In 1966 the unemployment rate varied from only 1 per cent in Spain (because of substantial emigration) to 6·5 per cent in Greece (also thanks to emigration). It is practically nil in Switzerland, in Sweden (0·5 per cent at most), in Denmark (0·4 per cent) and in the Netherlands, where the scarcity of labour is particularly felt and immigration has reached a very high level. In France, unemployment has increased since 1967 under the influence of the stabilization plan. For the Paris region alone it has officially reached 100,000 registered people, principally youths between 18 and 24 years of age, women, and wage-earners without special qualifications; underemployment is even more serious.

Standards of living

Generally speaking, the standard of living has risen in all European countries. Working conditions have improved – first, through the growing importance of mechanization which requires, on the whole, less muscular effort (though it increases nervous tension); and then through the reduction of working hours and through paid vacations.

The reduction of working hours is one of the oldest demands of workers throughout Europe. In France, the average workweek, 55 hours in 1913, was no more than 38·8 in 1936 (–30 per cent), the legal weekly maximum being 40 hours. Since 1945, though the legal limit has remained unchanged, the actual number of hours worked has increased in varying ways according to the situation in certain industries. The average working week in Paris is 46½ hours in the industrial sector and 41½ in the commercial and service sector, and in the provinces 50 and 44 hours, so that the legal reduction results in an increase in overtime, and the prolongation of active life compensates for the reduction of working hours. It has been said that the labourer today works as many hours as he did forty years ago. The actual workday in France is the longest of any country in Europe.

Salaries have, however, made progress since 1945, often under the pressure of strikes, but above all because of political measures creating full employment, which increases the scarcity of qualified labour. In Sweden, where there is a great shortage of labour, both quantitatively and qualitatively, the strongly organized trade unions guarantee an annual rise in wages and social advantages – for instance, assistance during periods of professional retraining. They watch over the whole disposition of labour and its adaptation to changing needs by helping workmen to improve their qualifications. Since 1938 a continuous dialogue between unions and employers has fixed annual agreements (every three years at the Volvo works) on wages, and the government exercises strong pressure in this direction on the highly centralized employers' organizations.

Great Britain adopted an incomes policy belatedly, ten years after Sweden. A National Incomes Commission created in 1962, and replaced in 1965 by a National Board for Prices and Incomes, opted in 1966 for a policy of the Swedish type. The Labour government wanted to keep the question of prices in the open, and thus to enable the Board to force firms to explain why they do not reduce their prices if their profits appear abnormally high.

The serious economic and social problems which arose in the Netherlands because of overpopulation after the Second World War led the government deliberately to keep wages below those of the other western countries in order to improve its export position. Thanks to this policy, full employment was maintained up to the 1960s; but since 1962 it has been necessary to raise the wage level several times. Here, too, the Swedish model has prevailed. Since 1963 the government has fixed ceiling prices for all industrial enterprises, and each firm which intends to increase its prices has to consult the interested ministry and obtain its agreement.

Italy provides a contrast with Sweden. There the labour force is overabundant, and the government is essentially concerned with

59, 60 Two aspects of the congestion of modern cities: a traffic jam in the Place de la Concorde, Paris, and *Business Prospers*, painting by Jean Dubuffet ▶

creating jobs so as to absorb the unemployed. Its principal effort, as we have already noted, is directed towards industrialization of the south.

As for wages, if one compares those actually earned in 1966 (including overtime, regular or output bonuses, lunch-vouchers, cost-of-living benefits), it emerges that the average hourly wage (in dollars) was $1.20 in Luxembourg, $1.15 in West Germany, $1.01 in Belgium, 95 cents in the Netherlands, 81 cents in France, and 69 cents in Italy. The highest wages are paid in the mining, petroleum, printing and metallurgy industries, while the lowest are in food, textiles and clothing. In any case, the range of wages has continually widened during the past ten years in France and even in Sweden. In 1966, 3,000,000 wage-earners in France earned less than 565 francs per month, but 17 per cent of higher salaried employees were paid more than 5,000 francs. In spite of rises obtained by the unions through the Grenelle agreements after the general strike of May–June 1968, one out of five French wage-earners was still earning less than 580 francs per month in industry and commerce until a substantial increase in the minimum guaranteed industrial wage (SMIG) was decided in October 1969.

The free enterprise system does not permit a real incomes policy. As Professor Titmus points out in his classical study, *Income Distribution and Social Change*, there are many 'natural advantages' and legal procedures which allow the directors and top executives of large corporations to escape the heavy taxes which they are required to pay by law: expense accounts, travel expenses and paid vacations, free homes and country houses, entertainment allowances, business lunches, cars and chauffeurs paid for by the company, etc. The inequality of wages and salaries among the various occupations, and especially between the sexes, remains an important problem.

Social change

Education is an essential factor in the improvement of the status of the lower classes, and around this subject there have been violent conflicts, not only in Europe but all over the world. It is a question of achieving a triple objective: (1) to obey the democratic principle of the equality of men by reducing advantages of birth as far as possible and giving the benefits of equal opportunity as a start to all; (2) to spread education so that culture shall not be the privilege of the few; and (3) to form the educated class of technicians increasingly demanded by our industrial civilization. Experience shows that the opportunities of achieving any particular social level are closely connected with the individual's original class status. Mobility is weakest at the top and the bottom of the ladder. The sons of the most favoured groups (higher management, the liberal professions, industrialists and large-scale tradesmen), and of the least favoured (labourers and farmworkers), are least likely to escape the social *milieu* of their fathers. Birth into an easy background allows a child to pursue his studies longer and increases his chances of remaining in the same social group; it gives him the assurance conferred by awareness of belonging to the ruling class and spares him worries about his future. As for the least fortunate, there are scholarships and maintenance grants which compensate for the lack of salary, but the distinction which has long been made between the scholarship boy and the heir of an old or wealthy family is not a myth, for it concerns not only money but differences of background. On the other hand, the Second World War led to the realization, even among the lower classes, that a more solid education and more extended studies are currently the principal – and the fairest – means of achieving a rise in social status and attaining both prestige and better material living conditions. Thus parents of all classes desire to use education as a means of helping their children avoid manual labour and ascend the social ladder. Hence the need to increase the number of educational establishments at all levels and to make study easier for all who desire it. In this way the composition of the ruling class is gradually modified. In fact, the leaders of economic and political life, i.e. the rulers of the nation, are nowadays recruited from the middle classes and the upper bourgeoisie. Two particularly suggestive examples will suffice: the heads of the three British political parties, including Labour (among whom there are several scholarship boys), are most often Public School boys from the dozen best-known colleges. In the higher ranks of the Civil Service and large firms, they predominate over grammar school boys and graduates of the new red-brick universities. This is why British history has been described as 'a succession of Balliol men'. In 1950, according to Anthony Sampson, of 1,045 high-ranking civil servants, 23 per cent had come from Public Schools (and 2 per cent of these from Winchester). At the same period, of 331 civil servants of the highest rank, 10 per cent were sons of civil servants, 10 per cent were sons of clergymen, 11 per cent were sons of schoolmasters, and 13 per cent (a little more than one in eight) were sons of manual labourers.

In France the executive staff of corporations and of public and private administrations are recruited from students of the classical schools of higher education: the Polytechnique, the School of Civil Engineering, and the National School of Administration. This is true also of the most important state institutions, such as the Council of State, the Inspectorate of Finance, and the Audit Office, and a growing proportion of directors and heads of large firms. Recruits to the 'grandes écoles' come from families of the liberal professions (15 per cent), and from the middle ranks of commerce and industry (23 per cent); the proportion from the working class is only 2 per cent, from tradesmen and the self-employed 10 per cent, and from farmers 4 per cent.

Most of the institutions developed since the British Education Act of 1944 have taken into consideration the principle formulated in the Declaration of Human Rights, promulgated in 1948 by the United Nations, which proclaims that 'everyone has the right to education, that it must be free at least at the elementary level, and that at that level it must be obligatory'. The rise of education can also be explained by the population explosion since the Second World War; this has necessitated new educational establishments and an increase in the number of students. Between 1955 and 1960, there were in western Europe 36,000,000 children of 5 to 9 years of age, 2,000,000 between 10 and 14, and 4,000,000 adolescents of 15 to 19. At the beginning of the 1950s, hundreds of thousands of children had to have schooling provided for them; a few years later, at the beginning of the 1960s, it was the universities which were affected by this population explosion and which proved to be totally inadequate.

Connected with the pressure of public opinion and increased population are the needs of industrial society for more and more specialized and sophisticated labour, for well-trained technicians capable of applying the latest technological innovations and of playing a growing role in basic, applied and technical research. Thus it is no longer simply the problem of literacy that has to be dealt with, as in preceding generations, but that of developing higher education and, consequently, of secondary education, which is the precondition for higher learning and has ceased to be the prerogative of the privileged few.

Public education is therefore one of the major tasks facing all governments. Everywhere in Europe, education is obligatory at least for children between 6 and 11 years, and, according to country, until 14, 15 or 16. Sometimes the state is in direct charge, sometimes there are private schools – most often confessional – which the state subsidizes and controls more or less effectively. In some countries (e.g., Great Britain), but by no means all, it is free. Questions of organization – the degree to which the natural sciences are displacing traditional curricula based on Greek and Latin, the number of years spent in school, the age and level at which children begin to specialize, the criteria for passing from one to another of the three traditional levels (primary, secondary and higher) – these are all extremely variable and are governed, in almost all countries, by examinations. Technical schools are also multiplying everywhere at all the various levels. Illiteracy has shrunk and disappeared in virtually all countries except for Portugal, where 70 per cent of the population over 7 years of age is illiterate, Greece with 17 per cent, and Spain where 70 per cent of the population over the age of 13 is also illiterate.

In the period 1960–63, the ratio of students preparing for higher education, i.e. the ratio between the numbers enrolled in the first year of schooling and in the classes for 18- and 19-year-olds, was 34 per cent in the United States, 7·3 per cent in the USSR, 8·5 per cent in the United Kingdom, 7·3 per cent in West Germany, 17·4 per cent in Belgium, 13·8 per cent in France, 6 per cent in Italy, and 4·6 per cent in the Netherlands. Since that time, the increase in the number of university students has been considerable; indeed, university education, too, has become a mass phenomenon. In France between 1960–61 and 1966–67, in the universities alone, the number rose from 214,673 to 499,442. In no country (and notably in France) does this increase bear any relationship to the quality of studies, particularly since the barriers to entry into universities have become minimal, or sometimes do not exist at all. The proof is the failure of the large majority of students who are unable to complete the normal course of studies. (In France this amounts to three-quarters.)

What is the social origin of these students whose numbers are growing so prodigiously? If one takes higher education in France as an example, in 1967 the percentage of students in relation to the total population of the same age was 4·6 for the children of agricultural labourers, farmers and wage-earners, 17·1 for those of industrial and commercial businessmen; 57 for the liberal professions, and 3·4 for factory workers; in other words, more than half of French students at this level belong to the middle or upper bourgeoisie and less than 10 per cent are of lower-class origin.

99

The effort to provide education at all levels is sometimes supplemented (as in the USSR and Yugoslavia) by the organization of correspondence colleges or evening classes, with the purpose of permitting adults to complete studies which they have been prevented from pursuing or forced to interrupt. This is already being done in France by the Conservatory of Arts and Professions and its extensions in the provinces. The provincial universities are also preparing to undertake this service, on the model of the university extension courses which have existed for a long time in Great Britain, Austria, Finland, Denmark (courses of five to six winter months), the Netherlands and Germany (where there are courses in more than fifty subjects). In Norway the project is just beginning.

These real improvements must not be underestimated, but the results remain largely unequal to the needs. It is estimated, for example, that the increase in the school-age population of London will require several hundreds of additional classes. There are clearly not enough teachers, and increasingly they are women; recruitment to the profession is difficult and sometimes of mediocre quality. The situation is the same in France and most other countries.

The general need to make education more democratic is thus being satisfied only slowly and incompletely. On the one hand, it remains very inferior in creating the graduates that industrial society requires, and on the other, it permits the existence, within the various classes, of social strata that remain in an astonishing state of intellectual underdevelopment. Finally, the persistent shortage of technical experts is made worse by the departure of research students, scholars and technicians attracted by the United States. Great Britain and Germany are particularly affected by this 'brain drain'.

CONCLUSION

The slogan attributed to the British Prime Minister, Harold Macmillan, in the late '50s – 'You never had it so good' – was perhaps true for certain voters, but certainly not for the great majority. Marxists claim that an increasingly large part of profits are being retained by employers, and that in recent years the workers' situation has grown worse; in conformity with Marxist dogma there will be a 'total pauperization' of the working class. The investigation made by two French economists, François Sellier and André Tiano, comes to the conclusion that 'total pauperization can be neither demonstrated nor denied in a completely scientific way'. But if pauperization is only relative, the real improvement in the standard of living cannot be questioned; nor can there be any doubt that a number of evils, which caused the working class deep suffering in the nineteenth century, have been palliated, if not done away with entirely. This has induced a change of climate made possible by the ability of industrial society to satisfy needs which grow in number but are standardized. Another factor favouring this change has been the policy of most governments on the stabilization of prices, full employment, wages and social security.

Does this mean that the workers' organizations are satisfied? Certainly not. There is no doubt that groups which used to be revolutionary – a few minorities apart – have become institutionalized and appear to be on the way towards integration in the new capitalist society, but they still demand increased opportunities for wage-earners and the improvement of their conditions; they claim effective participation in management and the right to a say in the earning of profits and their use. The worker wants to understand the aims of the business and the work he is ordered to do; he wants a higher wage which will assure him substantial personal savings. Above all, he believes that, in many cases, social legislation has gradually been drained of its substance and diverted from the intentions of its sponsors. Even though social legislation has improved, it still permits shocking inequalities which result from the absence of harmony between progressive social laws, which assure the workers a certain legal security, and the right of ownership which the proprietor possesses.

61 The brain drain:
a *Krokodil* cartoon (1965)

Under the pretext of ensuring the proper functioning of a firm, the law facilitates dismissals which may be arbitrary, since the workers are in no position to produce evidence that the firm's future is not in danger. This applies also to the refusal to re-employ a worker who has been laid off for alleged incompetence, when in fact the real motives are political.

As far as social security is concerned, the conservatives who accepted it only reluctantly are opposed to any attempt to turn it into a device for redistributing the national income, since unemployment insurance is, in effect, nothing but a means of redistributing wage earnings to the benefit of categories which have the greatest need. Factory committees, as well as the administration councils of social security funds, have a very limited role. Nationalized industries have to obey the ministries in charge, particularly the finance ministry, which force them to give benefits to private enterprises in the form of sizable preferential tariffs. In Great Britain and the Scandinavian countries, factory councils have become the employers' monopoly because workers show little interest in them; it is perhaps only in the Netherlands that they operate with a normal collaboration of both sides. In West Germany, co-management is marking time; the working class, disillusioned and more preoccupied with comfort than responsibilities, is satisfied with a share in the profits.

III CHANGES IN SOCIETY

The extraordinary mobility of the population of Europe during the past twenty-five years is best examined as a function of three universal phenomena: mass production, the rural exodus, and the urbanization taking place in all countries – whether new or old and whether overindustrialized or underdeveloped.

The active population, and particularly the wage-earning sector, has been increasing everywhere, though at an unequal rate. (Between 1955 and 1965 the increase in France was 3·3 per cent as compared with 12 per cent in West Germany.) In relation to the total population, the number of workers in the United Kingdom was 92 per cent in 1950 and 92·8 per cent in 1964; in West Germany the figures for the same years were 68·6 and 77·4 per cent; in Belgium 71·5 and 71·7 per cent; in Norway 67·5 and 77·4 per cent; in France 64·3 and 71·3 per cent; and in Italy 54·7 and 64·2 per cent. More than a third of the wage-earners were women.

This phenomenon was accompanied by very rapid changes within each of the three sectors into which the economy is usually broken down, but principally by the decrease in the agricultural population. Between 1954 and 1966 the agricultural sector in France dropped from 28·2 to 17 per cent; in West Germany from 24·9 in 1958 to 11 per cent in 1968; in Italy from 39·9 to 24 per cent in 1966; in the United Kingdom from 8 to 3·5 per cent. In Switzerland it was 11·6 per cent in 1960 and in Belgium 6 per cent in 1966. The industrial sector, in the same period, rose in France from 37·1 to 41·1 per cent; in West Germany from 42·9 to 49 per cent; in Italy from 27·1 to 41 per cent; in the United Kingdom it reached 47 per cent in 1964; in Switzerland it was as high as 51 per cent in 1960, and in Belgium 45 per cent in the same year. As for the 'third' sector (comprising mainly services), it progressed in France during the same period from 34·7 to 39·2 per cent; in West Germany from 32·5 (in 1958) to 37·5 per cent; in Italy from 27·8 to 31 per cent; in the United Kingdom it reached 48 per cent in 1964, in Switzerland 38·9 per cent in 1960 and in Belgium 47 per cent in 1966.

For the whole of the EEC countries, the first sector (mining, fishing and agriculture) comprised only 16 per cent of the working population in 1966, the second (industry) 43 per cent, and the third 39 per cent (compared with the same figures for the USSR – 38, 30 and 32, and the USA – 5, 33 and 58). Whereas the total population grew by 12·4 per cent between 1954 and 1966, the urban population gained 13·8 per cent and the rural population, since 1930 no more than 31 per cent of the working population, lost 5·6 per cent.

It is very difficult to discover precisely how many peasants own their own farms; most of the published statistics are concerned almost exclusively with the sizes of holdings and it is well known that many large estates are divided for farming purposes into small or medium-sized lots assigned to tenant-farmers or sharecroppers. This is true of many British estates which are often larger than 2,500 acres, but of which 38 per cent are rented to tenant-farmers. The same situation exists in southern Italy, Spain and Portugal. France, with its reputation of being a land of small landowners and small enterprises, does in fact have a great number of them; but often these are inadequate patches of land whose owners have to lease other acreage, or work in the industries of the nearest town, in order to survive. In reality, 4 per cent of the large farms in the former département of Seine-et-Oise account for half of the cultivated soil, and in most other départements they comprise 20 and 24 per cent of the whole. Taking western Europe as a whole, large farms are rare and their sizes variable. In West Germany only 0·2 per cent of farm holdings are larger than 250 acres; in France 1·4 per cent, in Italy 0·5 per cent, in the Netherlands 0·1 per cent and in Belgium 0·2 per cent. In Portugal, of 800,000 farms, 700,000 are no larger than 15 acres at most. In general, those less than 25 acres belong in France to 54 per cent of the number of farmers, in the Netherlands to 67·6 per cent, in Belgium to 81·7 per cent, and in West Germany to 80 per cent. The large farms (125 acres and over) belong respectively to 4·6 per cent of the farmers in France, 0·8 per cent in the Netherlands and Belgium, 2·6 per cent in West Germany.

The general tendency is towards concentration into farms with an area of over 125 acres. A survey undertaken in France in 1967 showed that, from 1955 to 1963, the number of farms had fallen from 2,286,000 to about 1,900,000, i.e. a reduction of 26 per cent in eight years. By the end of 1968 the total had fallen to 1,640,000 and it is estimated that the number will eventually drop to 1,000,000 (2·5 per cent a year), for most of them are small units (69 per cent of serviceable soil) of less than 25 acres each, which is considered to be the minimum profitable size. The associations of land development and rural settlement (SAFER), created in 1963, are charged with buying plots and building up agricultural establishments with an income sufficient for family farming. The Mansholt plan and other current trends (in France in 1969, for example) will bring about an even greater decrease in the number of farms, most of which are unprofitable.

The course of development in Belgium is similar. Here it is estimated that 4 per cent of farms disappear each year, but 66 per cent of farmers do not own their own land. In West Germany, the pace is less rapid: 6 per cent of farms disappeared between 1945 and 1960. In Italy the rural population diminished by 10 per cent between 1956 and 1967, but estate-farming still accounts for 82 per cent. In the Netherlands, on the other hand, government policy aims at the creation of large farms by granting a pension to small farmers who retire at the age of 65.

This development reveals two other world-wide trends, which are rapidly gathering pace: the decreasing share of agriculture in gross national income, and the growing significance of the rural exodus. Agriculture accounts for less than 5 per cent of national income in Great Britain and Sweden, between 6 and 10 per cent in Belgium, France, West Germany, the Netherlands and Switzerland, and 10 to 20 per cent in Denmark and Italy; it is no more than 25 per cent in Ireland, and 25 to 30 per cent in the relatively underdeveloped countries of southern Europe – Greece, Spain and Portugal.

Agricultural labour in western Europe amounts to less than 25 million man-hours per year, i.e. one-quarter of all labour. This drop in the labour force has not, however, prevented the growth of output, except in Greece, Turkey and Portugal, where the rate of population increase is much higher than that of per capita production.

Thus it is not surprising that the peasants of France, Italy and Germany should be uneasy. This is caused by their indebtedness (for purchases of equipment) and by the uncertainties arising from the Common Market; it is sometimes translated into violent agitation. However, there have also been other more positive reactions. Since 1945 farmers have recognized their need for technical training, and have increasingly shown interest in experiment and research. They have created cooperatives to look after the quality-control, stocking and packaging of their products, as well as the concentration of sales operations. They have sought to modernize and improve their methods and equipment through mechanization, and have established channels for the merchandising and export of fruits and vegetables, a branch of agriculture in which there is frequently overproduction. In sum, they are now aware that agriculture has to adapt itself to a market economy by working out cost prices, as the farmers of the most advanced countries (particularly Denmark) and the industrialists do.

Nevertheless, legislation everywhere has been concerned with the peasants, who have benefited from the sympathy of conservative parties; the result has been a multiplication of protective measures. In France the laws have favoured medium-sized farms by facilitating loans from agricultural credit banks and by the creation of SAFER. Since 1945–46, measures have been passed to limit the powers of landowners in favour of the farmer, who now has the automatic right to renew his lease or to receive indemnity in case of repossession by the landlord.

62 Publicizing the glamour of colour television

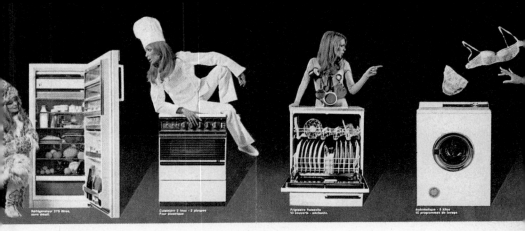

63 The new necessities of life, according to advertising

This protection of the peasants has been supplemented in all countries by price supports, increased import tariffs, export subsidies and limitations on output. As a consequence the difference between internal and import prices has become considerable: sometimes 40 per cent, often between 5 and 20 per cent. This is an important factor in raising the cost of living and contributes to the high level of cost prices in industry.

In spite of improvement in the peasants' lot, the disparity of incomes has been growing, for the changes enumerated above favour those with the greatest volume of sales, and not the poorest. This is one of the reasons for the above-mentioned regrouping of farms, the increase in mechanization and the application of techniques which, while employing fewer workers, raise production levels. It is also the reason for the decrease in cereal-growing, for the peasant now specializes in high-priced products which make it possible for him to compete with overseas producers.

Nevertheless, there remain a great number of farms so small that their resources are insufficient for them to participate in the general rise of the standard of living, despite the fact that agricultural products still represent a quarter or a half of consumers' expenses in all countries.

One result of the relative decline of agriculture is an exodus from the countryside. It does not affect so much farmers as agricultural workers, smallholders and their children, principally the young who suffer from having neither independence nor standing, and whose standard of living is low. The movement has been accelerated not so

107

much by distaste for working on the land and the attraction of industrial work, as by the irregularity of a life that is often miserable, and the lack of any guarantees in the event of illness and old age. What the peasant seeks, like all other wage-earners, is security, an economic level on a par with the industrial workers'. He will often take the position of a low-grade civil servant rather than manual labour. In the case of women, the inducement is above all the attraction of city life, with its possibilities of a job and of free time after work, but it is also a question of prestige.

In France, one-fifth of the agricultural population left the land between 1954 and 1962, but the trend is similar in Great Britain, where the already small number of farmworkers has decreased yet again by 25 per cent. In Switzerland, depopulation affects mainly the mountainous areas: from 16·8 in 1950, the percentage of agricultural workers dropped to 10·3 in 1960, many moving to lower-lying regions. Though the Alpine exodus is less catastrophic in Austria, the population has been shifting since 1945 towards the agglomeration of Vienna and the industrial valleys, except in the Vorarlberg and the southern part of the Tyrol where the birth-rate is high and tourism provides substantial resources. Between 1934 and 1961, the proportion of agricultural workers dropped from 36 to 23 per cent, but here, too, it was the small unprofitable farms that disappeared. In the Netherlands, the percentage of farmers and stock-raisers dropped from 82 per cent in 1954 to 49 per cent in 1965. In Luxembourg 2–3,000 peasants from the poor country in the north and east have left each year for the towns of neighbouring countries. In the same way, the category of peasant-workers, who divide their time between farm labour and factory work (common in West Germany and France), is tending to disappear in favour of exclusively industrial work.

We have already dealt with the numerous measures which have improved the situation of the industrial worker. But one of the most noteworthy features of our times is the rapid progress of the so-called third sector – that is, the sector comprising all non-manual labour, including transport, which does not actually produce new goods; in other words, the 'service industries' and the 'white-collar workers'. There are many differences and a great variety of social ranks within this category, even if we exclude 'managers' (i.e. higher echelons of the public administration, business executives, and members of the liberal professions who, although salaried, have creative and decision-making responsibilities, and form a group apart). Outside of these, the third sector includes domestic servants, shop assistants, office employees (typists, bank clerks, insurance agents), junior civil servants, many of whom are women, small dealers, and middle-grade executive staffs. The rise of these work-categories, different as they are, is characteristic of affluent and developed societies. Generally speaking, though the contrast in the mode of life between employees and manual workers has become less marked, the classic criterion of social stratification is dress: the white-collar worker considers himself superior to the roughly dressed manual labourer.

The third sector has grown with the progress of industrialization and administration, in which the division of labour creates many new positions. It is essentially urban. The Paris region, for instance, contains 49 per cent of the nation's engineers, 70 per cent of industrial research workers, 55 per cent of office workers, 35 per cent of students. Third-sector workers are distinguished not only by their dress, but also by their housing (which is generally more comfortable and better looked after), by their mode of life, their desire (particularly among women) to keep up with the whims of fashion, and by an education which is usually of a higher level (at least technically) than that of the other two sectors.

In Switzerland and West Germany, the third sector absorbs between 50 and 80 per cent of those who leave the first sector; in Italy between 40 and 50 per cent; in Spain and Greece between 30 and 40 per cent; in Great Britain, Sweden (where it has been the only source of new employment), France, Belgium and the fairly recently industrialized Netherlands, virtually the total of those lost by the first and second sectors have passed into the third. By and large, this influx into the third sector can be explained by dislike of manual labour and the feeling of men (and especially women) that, by entering the third sector, they are moving into a higher social category. The income difference varies but is generally not negligible, even though many specialized labourers receive higher wages than a number of lower-grade white-collar workers. But it is not money, so much as other factors, which are decisive. Most third-sector workers, for example, are paid a monthly salary rather than weekly wages; they work in cleaner conditions and enjoy greater stability of employment. Thus they have greater security and do not feel like 'proletarians'. Those who belong to the 'staff', even the lower grades, have possibilities of advancement, whereas the labourer cannot hope to see his situation ever improve so greatly that he can fully enjoy the advantages of a consumer society. This results on the part of white-collar workers in a tendency to save and to acquire durable goods (sometimes by credit-purchase and instalment-plan, particularly in the case of housing, electric household utensils, televisions, automobiles, etc.).

The political attitude of third-sector workers also is different from that of workers in the other sectors. They are not likely to read the working-class or Socialist press, preferring bourgeois newspapers and magazines which feature photographs of stars and celebrities – a taste of luxury which enables them to identify themselves with the higher social strata. They are much less inclined than manual workers to vote for left-wing parties.

Within this new social stratum one can witness the rapid progress of middle- or high-level technologists, who enjoy a salary that offers them a different way of life from those with smaller incomes. In the general trend towards 'embourgeoisement', this class has become increasingly significant and takes pains to distinguish itself above all from manual workers and low-salaried employees (many of whom are nevertheless also white-collar workers). It is this class which strives

64 A trans-Europe luxury express

THE GROWING IMPORTANCE
OF LEISURE

65, 66, 67, 68 Top, holiday advertising for air travel; above, Swiss Railways publicity; above right, Soviet tourists posing near Tower Bridge, London; right, Nordic tourists on the Spanish Steps, Rome

most to procure higher education for its children in the hope of seeing them become part of the 'establishment'. It is also the class most given to expensive vacations and distant voyages, and which seeks 'prestige' homes with elegant furniture. This 'upper lower class' is in an equivocal situation; it is salaried and therefore dependent, but it lives like the bourgeoisie. Its dilemma was brought to light, in France, by the strikes of spring 1968, when the CGC, the organization which groups the high-level staffs of public and private administrations, joined with the trade unions in demanding participation in co-management, greater security of employment and higher pay. Thus it constitutes an intermediary social stratum, conscious of its important part in the country's economic life. It feels that its interests do not always coincide with those of the ruling class, which it envies and with which it would like to be able to identify itself. Because they enjoy high salaries, its members are not concerned with social inequality (on the contrary, they seek to distinguish themselves from those with lower incomes), but with the difficulties of social climbing and the social standing for which they are so avid. They do not oppose the system of private property, and show little interest in politics, but they have learnt that on occasion they may have interests in common with the workers.

In several traditionalist countries, such as Great Britain, Belgium, Spain, Portugal, the Netherlands and Italy, the old aristocracy continues to play a part and to enjoy fortunes that are often considerable. In Scotland and England there are still very large estates, preserved in spite of heavy taxes and high death-duties. Members of this class enjoy an undisputed prestige which assures them a kind of priority in the most impressive public positions (embassies, high army commands, the top jobs at least in certain public administrations where it is rare not to find a large number of titles) and in elected office, as well as on the boards of large firms which seek historic names. These people form a narrow, closed caste, which intermarries among itself, except in Great Britain where sons-in-law of more modest birth are acceptable so long as they are rich and influential. This aristocracy of birth and money constitutes an international European-American upper class whose way of life has become the exception in Europe, and there is a tendency for it to blend with the other upper class which has emerged elsewhere through the fusion of the aristocracy of birth with the *haute bourgeoisie*.

In reality, the ruling class of most western European countries forms a plutocracy composed of a few thousand individuals disposing of fortunes in the millions. Anthony Sampson reports that in Great Britain in 1962, 3,000 people had an income (after tax) of more than £20,000, and 15,000 had over £10,000. Moreover, 1 per cent of British adults (among whom the aristocracy were a relatively small number) owned 43 per cent of the total net capital, while 6,000,000 had an income not much higher, on average, than £500 a year.

The general standard of living has, nevertheless, risen in all social classes. The growth of consumption since 1945 has been greater than in any comparable period. (In Great Britain it has increased an average of 2 per cent every year.) In 1960, for the first time in France, expenditure on food absorbed less than half the average income of the working man. The female worker or employee, freed by labour-saving devices from heavy domestic duties, and entertained by the record-player, radio and television, takes better care of her clothes and person and is scarcely distinguishable in appearance from women of the more privileged classes. The proliferation of tourist agencies and the organization of foreign tours and cruises offer a wide variety of opportunities at varying prices (some of them very low), which attract multitudes of people who are inquisitive and looking for escape. Camping activities, the chain of youth hostels, and the various youth and student associations offer study and recreation trips which used to be the privilege of the wealthy. For all classes the result has been a rush towards nature and the open air, a thirst for knowledge of foreign places. These annual vacations of several weeks, which the employee or worker may dream of all year long, do not preclude week-end trips (most firms and administrations having gone over to the five-day week), as can be seen from the increasing number of week-end cottages and automobiles. The prodigious success of paper backs is also evidence of the need for escape or intellectual improvement. Participation in sports (swimming, football, hockey, underwater fishing, parachuting, horseback riding, skiing and water-skiing), some of which were considered not very long ago to be the preserve of the aristocracy and bourgeoisie, has become popular because of its moderate cost. Sailing and motorboats have also become more important to the middle classes, while the old sports of shooting and fishing continue to be in vogue.

A whole policy of extramural cultural development is pursued by numerous municipalities with a greater or lesser degree of state assistance. Governments undertake to organize leisure activities, recreation, and the acquisition of skills outside of school, i.e. to make it possible for workers with free time – due to vacations and reduced working-hours – to fill their time judiciously. Such undertakings include the construction of swimming-pools, stadiums, sports-grounds, vacation villages, youth hostels, and cultural, social and theatre centres. We may also include in this category regional parks in France (e.g. Vanoise, Mercantour, Aigoual) and Great Britain; the 'community houses' in the *Land* of Hessen in Germany; the leisure-centres created in Zurich, which may be considered as models. Among other examples are the regional park at St Amand les Eaux in France; the artificial lake at Dijon; the development of woods around Amsterdam; the regional park in the Lea Valley, where all the equipment necessary for recreational activities will be made available. The taste for theatre is catered for unequally: in Germany there are 178 theatres and opera houses in 102 towns with a capacity of 1,030 per 10,000 inhabitants; Czechoslovakia and Norway have a capacity only slightly lower, whereas in France the ratio is only one theatre per 52,000 inhabitants. Visits to museums, national palaces and historic châteaux or stately homes have also greatly increased.

The press, concentrated in a very few hands, provides the principal, if not the only, reading matter of the majority of Europeans, particularly in France, where a taste for reading rarely survives the school-years. Only 12 per cent of French adults were enrolled in a library in 1960. Whereas the public libraries in London lent more than 40,000,000 books to 3,257,000 people in 1961, in Paris 3,071,000 books were borrowed by 1,750,000 people. Moreover, 58 per cent of the French population never bought a book at all in 1962.

What, then, does 'popular culture' amount to? In the past the working class had an autonomous culture of its own: it had its own language and customs, regional costume, a traditional history transmitted orally and through the popular literature disseminated by pedlars. Today this has become a 'folklore' which is artificially revived, solely for tourists. Mass culture has replaced it with the imitation of styles spread by the cinema and strip cartoons; a literature of sub-mediocre, if not infantile, quality, such as is diffused by the high-circulation newspapers; romantic novels of extreme vulgarity; adventure, crime and spy novels or science fiction. The result has

69 Helsinki city theatre

70 Philharmonic concert
hall, in West Berlin

71 Below, the
contradictions of modern
life: cartoon by Sempé

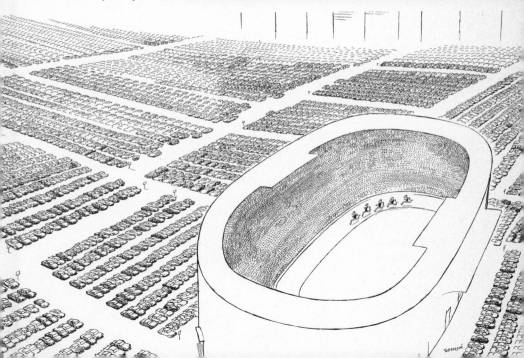

72, 73 Pop culture. Left, Carnaby Street, pop fashion centre in London; right, a view of the 100,000 fans at a 1969 pop concert on the Isle of Wight

been to cut the working class off from the literature intended for the extremely limited 'cultivated' class. Hence there is a divorce between the new culture of the people and the 'true' culture, visible, for example, in the lack of understanding of all innovative work: that of Le Corbusier with his extraordinary inventive genius, or of many contemporary painters who are hardly recognized in their own countries. This separation is revealed by the decadence of contemporary Soviet art; the rich and promising artistic culture which flowered after 1917 was followed by a pseudo-classical art, outstripped in the west, but preferred by the Soviet people. On the other side, the cultivated class tends to enclose itself in a hermetic art and literature, whose 'quality', confused with originality, can be appreciated only by a few initiates. In the same way, dance music, jazz and popular songs have a far greater public than classical music.

116

The structure of society has been largely transformed by the ascent of new social groups, and also by the changes which have taken place in the various consumer categories. If the nineteenth century was the century of the 'conquering bourgeoisie', the twentieth is that of the 'dominant bourgeoisie'. No doubt the process of levelling has tended to eradicate the more shocking material distinctions that used to exist among the different classes; but the improvement in standards of living has been distributed no less unequally. The increase in wage-earners' buying power, taking into account the rise in the cost of living, is calculated since 1950 at 8 per cent in the Netherlands, 6 per cent in West Germany, 3 to 5 per cent in France (depending on whether unmarried people or heads of families are concerned), 4 per cent in Luxembourg, 3·5 per cent in Italy, 3 per cent in Belgium, and only 2 per cent in Great Britain. Among the developed countries of industrial Europe, France has the most evident social inequality: the 10 per cent of the richest people have retained 75 per cent of national income since 1954, whereas the poorest 10 per cent received only 4·8 per cent. In Germany and the Netherlands, the corresponding groups received 30 and 7·7 per cent. It is only in the Netherlands and Sweden that the three groups comprising the poorest 30 per cent of the population are assured of the most equitable portion of national income. Whereas in countries dominated by Labour less than 45 per cent of national income goes to the privileged 20 per cent, in France and West Germany they receive more than 50 per cent. Even in Sweden the process of equalization seems to be reversing itself.

Differences in the standard of living among the western countries remain very substantial. The lack of uniformity in statistical methods, differences of environment (urban or rural), and variations of taxation make it difficult to compare household consumption. But it is evident, on the basis of monetary parity, that there are substantial discrepancies in the non-agricultural sector of the economy, excluding the professions and managing groups: to take only one example, the average family in Luxembourg has a buying power of 168 as compared with the Italian family's 100.

The result of this sizable inequality of income is a great inequality of consumption. The average food budget of a French family of the upper management group is only 45 per cent higher than that of an employee's family, whereas its other expenditures are 116 per cent higher. In other words, it is the type of consumption which shows the greatest variability. Household comforts are most equally distributed in Great Britain, where three in five homes have a vacuum-cleaner, two in five a washing-machine, one in three a refrigerator and nine out of ten a television; the number of automobiles rose from 2,500,000 in 1951 to 6,000,000 in 1961.

This inequality shows, contrary to common belief, that the dominant classes are more powerful today than before. The reason is that they have adopted a new strategy and new techniques, which are infinitely more effective than those of the nineteenth century. The policy of authoritarianism or brutal repression (Henry Ford said: 'What one expects from the worker is not to understand, but to carry out orders') has given place – except in a few lagging countries – to a more adroit policy which relies on much less authoritarian relations within a firm than formerly. Through improvements, not negligible in themselves but affecting only details – such as paid vacations, social undertakings supported by the firm, holiday homes, productivity bonuses, proliferation of categories and pay inequalities that divide the workers – the wage-earners' attention is diverted from the fundamental problems raised by their place in society. While keeping a watch over all expressions of political opinion and eliminating 'subversive elements', the employers organize a system of internal promotion which raises the workers' hopes of becoming 'executives'. But the preponderance of employers' authority is due above all else to the division of the working class into rival political parties and unions which practise one-upmanship and wrangle over membership, in spite of the fact that their development is noticeably towards the moderation of demands.

74 Erotic advertisement of the 1960s

In the eastern countries, too, the rise of industry has brought rapid urbanization in its train. As Pierre George observes, 'industry has been the motor of urbanization'. Of the total Soviet population, 54 per cent, principally in Europe, is urban (as compared with 80·8 per cent in Great Britain, 71·1 per cent in West Germany, 55·9 per cent in France). Between 1926 and 1958, 43,000,000 people from the land (an annual average of 1,340,000) came to live in towns; 31·7 per cent of these towns have more than 100,000 inhabitants, and eight of them have more than a million. As we have noted, this is a general phenomenon resulting from the centralizing tendencies of the modern state, the progress of industry and transport which demand an increased number of services in quantity and quality. The consequences are familiar: loss of work-hours in travel over long distances, higher mortality, more illegitimate births, delinquents, etc. The town-country antithesis and urban concentration produce unquestionable disadvantages. Thus the problem of land development has arisen in the USSR, as in the west. The aim is to create work-towns out of little villages, where the bonds between industry and agriculture can more easily develop. These are to become 'growth points' (the concept of François Perroux, which the Soviets were the first to understand) with a minimum of 60–80,000 inhabitants, the optimum number being 250,000. On the other hand, the large centres burst out and extend into the suburbs and conurbations, like Volgograd which stretches along 45 miles of the Volga, or Moscow where twenty-four satellite towns have been created within a radius of 12 miles to house a million inhabitants. (Compare London with its sixteen satellite towns of 100,000 inhabitants, and Paris surrounded by 200 *communes* with a total of 3,000,000 inhabitants.) Large population centres are still very dispersed in the USSR; even today only 31·6 per cent of the total population lives east of the Urals.

Controlled and planned urban development is favoured in the Soviet Union by the absence of land speculation, a result of the prohibition of private ownership of the land and the lower cost of building by comparison with the west. However, city-planners run into the same difficulties as their western colleagues in creating urban communities in large areas with no past. They try to erase the old distinction between town and country by the interpenetration of new towns and the countryside, a process which has been made possible by improved transport.

119

ASPECTS OF LIFE IN THE USSR

75, 76, 77 Top, newly built areas of Volgograd; above, communal television room in
Moscow block of flats; right, Molodezhnoye Café, Volgograd

The Soviet town is very different from the town in the west. It is essentially an industrial centre and an administrative and cultural transmission point, a node for the collection and distribution of products. Its population is composed of workers and state employees. Its buildings, because of war destruction and the dilapidated condition of old houses, are almost all recent. Its structure is also completely different from its western counterparts.

A survey undertaken in the eastern countries by the International Union of Architects, to discover the inhabitants' wishes and needs, made it possible to work out a plan, in conformity with Communist principles, which avoids class distinctions (hence the absence of differentiated residential neighbourhoods) and respects historical centres or buildings of artistic significance in the old cities. Dwellings conform to strict norms based on the number of people per family. From the start, the dwellings were grouped into independent neighbourhoods, equipped with commercial, medical and cultural services, and coupled with the factory where the inhabitants work, the two being divided by a simple green zone (parks, gardens, sports fields, planted traffic axes). This is the way the increase of 60,000,000 in the urban population in thirty years were housed. In order to avoid loss of time, the towns were sited as close as possible to sources of raw material and transport facilities. The commercial centre is small, since there is no private enterprise and those concerned with commerce are few. In order to speed things up, extensive use was made of industrial prefabrication, the least expensive type of construction being the medium-rental four- or five-storey house containing forty to fifty apartments, which can be built in five or six months rather than three years. Concrete panels weighing 120 lb. are used (whereas an equivalent quantity of bricks would weigh a ton). Sometimes, especially between 1945 and 1955, these uniform concrete surfaces were slightly varied.

Communal services (such as shops selling prepared or semi-prepared meals, and laundromats) have been expanded in order to free women from heavy, time-consuming, domestic work. But Soviet towns are colourless and gloomy. There are no illuminated advertisements in shops; the exteriors of houses are neglected; often rebuilding is incomplete and wooden houses continue to exist side by side with new blocks of flats.

78 Soviet cartoon showing inadequacy of modern transport

Диаграмма роста одного микрорайона.

Рисунок Е. ГУРОВА

79 The worker threatened by automation: from *Krokodil* (1965)

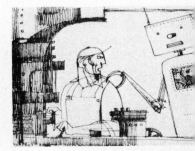

New problems have been raised by the growing differentiation in methods of production and professional qualifications. More and more, these force members of the same family out of the factory associated with the town, to work at centres some distance away. Automation makes factories even more specialized and reduces their personnel requirements; at the same time the possibilities of motor transport and the use of new sources of energy create new conditions, which both demand and make possible the build-up of urban transport. On the other hand, nearby factories pollute the atmosphere, making it unwholesome and disagreeable, so that the present tendency (as also, for example, in Switzerland and the USA) is to separate them from the residential areas and to make changes in industrial architecture. Residential quarters are transferred to the suburbs and satellite towns, preferably near wooded zones so that their parks and gardens are linked with trees. The first satellite town created at Kriukovo, 20 miles from Moscow, is surrounded by a forest, along the edge of which the schools and children's playgrounds were built.

In 1960, development of an experimental neighbourhood was started south-west of Moscow on a site of 600 acres, of which 100 are planted. The design is for 4,500 apartments to house 15,000 people in units for families of 2, 3, 4 and 5 members. Everything is prefabricated and the blocks are grouped in sections, each with its own schools, restaurants, crèche, club, sports-fields, garden, common household services, pharmacy, post office, savings bank, administrative buildings, as well as a commercial centre, theatre, cinemas and hotels. The houses are provided with garbage disposal and bathrooms; efforts have been made to orient dwellings towards more light and greenery, each town having a green belt.

Developments such as these are as yet the exception and many Soviet citizens still have to live in extremely cramped quarters. But it is obvious that the outskirts are, and will be, better developed than the town-centres; groups of buildings will be less close together, blocks will be separated by parks. Nevertheless, the satellite towns of Moscow are the most successful example of Soviet town-planning to date. Since the distances are considerable, they are linked by rapid electric trains radiating 20 to 30 miles from the centre and serving the *dachy*, the week-end and summer houses which are numerous in the north, north-east and north-west sectors. This is true also of Leningrad's new satellite towns and the city centre, served by an underground railway constructed beneath the Neva delta.

The main problem in the coutryside is the regrouping of villages whose inhabitants demand not only more comfort but also cultural and social centres. The regrouping of *kolkhozes* will give them a new aspect: there will be a concentrated nucleus instead of ribbon development, the villages being assembled either into ten or fifteen towns composed of semi-detached houses with adjoining fields, or into blocks of several storeys with interior passageways. This rearrangement of villages will tend to reduce the differences between the worker's and the peasant's way of life. Although there is less inequality in the USSR than elsewhere in the inhabitants' mode of living, it is still true that workers and peasants, who comprise by far the great majority of the Soviet population, form two separate categories distinguished even today by different mentalities. The workers, associated in unions, have adapted themselves easily to the new economic organization, whereas many peasants retain the outlook of small proprietors. But the differences are decreasing, owing to the growing mechanization of agriculture, which makes the working conditions of each much more similar.

There exists, however, a new social stratum, whose numbers have been greatly augmented through industrialization. These are the graduates and technicians, the doctors and people employed in the economy (11,000,000 as against 2,500,000 in 1940) – engineers, architects, teachers (6,000,000), scientific researchers (2,500,000), statisticians, *sovkhoz* directors, factory administrators, and officers – who constitute a virtual 'third sector' with a political and social role that has become increasingly important. It was feared in the USSR that, in the long run, this stratum might constitute a new bourgeoisie of technocrats, with a privileged position. To prevent this was the purpose of reforms carried out in 1958; while retaining differences in pay, and thus in standards of living, these made obligatory a probationary work period of two years, between the end of secondary studies and entry into university or technical schools, in order to filter out access to advanced education. Other factors making for equality are the uniformity of housing (the size of which depends on the number of members in a family) and its low cost, plus the low cost of essential food and clothing. Of course, higher salaries make it possible to acquire scarce goods and to enjoy more expensive recreation, but the limitation of property and inheritance to personal real estate and belongings, plus the impossibility of capitalizing on savings, mean that inheritance cannot lead to the creation of a capitalist class.

The People's Democracies

Born after the expulsion of German troops and their allies, the People's Democracies passed through a transition period of varying length during the first years following the end of operations. Since 1946, however, all took the path of collectivization of the means of production, and moved, progressively, towards a real collectivization of the economy. This transformed their social structure so profoundly that their physiognomy was completely changed. Nevertheless, the weight of the past has given each its own characteristics. They are affected by regional traditions, which are so powerful in agricultural societies; the diversity of languages, religions and customs; the unequal distribution of natural resources; and the more or less rapid progress of their individual economies. Having started out from different points, they have by no means attained the same standard of living. Except for East Germany and Czechoslovakia, which were already strongly industrialized, all these countries were still under a semi-colonial or quasi-feudal regime, with a preponderant and often illiterate rural population. War destruction and the influx of refugees from the east were additional factors in delaying reorganization of their structures. Hence inequalities of income and prices, and consequently of standards of living, still remain significant. The Soviet model, which was almost forty years in advance, has been imitated as a whole, but with variations and, generally speaking, a much greater flexibility, particularly in recent years.

By and large, agrarian reforms, more or less completely realized, have made it possible to improve the peasants' lot through the reduction of obligatory deliveries, the raising of production prices in 1960, irrigation and drainage works, bonuses favouring the development of specified crops, the grant of greater autonomy to cooperatives with freedom to make contracts with industrial firms, the concession of tax-exemptions to the most productive units, and the increased number of tractors and other machinery put at the disposal of farmers.

In East Germany, crafts and retail trade continue to exist (20 per cent as against 80 per cent of state-controlled business). When he does not belong to a cooperative, the craftsman or shopkeeper remains the proprietor of his workshop and machinery or his shop; he receives a stock of merchandise in exchange for a bond. In Poland the private craftsman, considered as complementary to the socialized economy, benefits from a fixed tax and reductions if he invests or takes on apprentices for training.

The result has been a complete reshaping of the social structure. The agricultural population of Poland dropped from 70 per cent in 1931 to 56 per cent in 1950 and 48 per cent in 1960; the industrial sector, however, suffers from a labour shortage. In Czechoslovakia, half of the working population is in industrial employment, and agriculture is short of hands in spite of appeals for female labour (which is increasing); the agricultural population dropped from 70 per cent in 1938 to 48 per cent in 1960. In Hungary the rural population fell from 60·8 per cent in 1940 to 48 per cent in 1949, and the industrial population rose from 17·7 to 24·7 per cent. In Rumania the industrial population has risen from 12 to 18·2 per cent, a lower proportion than that of the other Socialist countries, and the agricultural population dropped from 74 to 58 per cent. In Poland the industrial sector, which comprised 12 per cent of the working population in 1931 and 20 per cent in 1951, now comprises more than a third. In Bulgaria, the industrial population totals 122,000 workers, 34 per cent of whom are in mining and heavy industry.

For these reasons the urban population has greatly increased. Old towns have been remodelled and enlarged. Twin cities and entirely new urban centres have been built along the lines adopted by all town-planners in eastern Europe: the pre-war style co-exists with buildings inspired by the western example. Entirely new development centres (e.g., Nova Huta near Cracow; Eisenhütte, formerly Stalin-stadt; Donaujvaros; Brasov New Town), or old ones reconstructed and often renamed (e.g., Zlin, now Gottwaldow), have multiplied or have been considerably extended. Historical centres and buildings of artistic interest, such as the old Hanseatic town of Rostock, Warsaw and Dresden, have been faithfully reconstructed as they were before their destruction.

The system of authoritarian planning has become much more pliant in the post-Stalin era. The plans set up by Gosplan are no longer imperatives but only frameworks of orientation, which fix the objectives of key industries and stimulants to encourage production. The period of liberalization in Czechoslovakia under Dubcek resulted in the creation of multiple cooperatives which managed hotels, restaurants and cafés, and the directing organs were elected by the members of the cooperative and controlled by a committee of consumers and customers. Productive enterprises also were granted a certain autonomy of management, and were grouped into consortia responsible for a specific branch of production, with a director whose task was the coordination of plans, investment and supplies. These consortia were free to sign contracts with their clients, and all that came under higher authority was the annual plans. Each enterprise was at liberty to seek credit and to make investments, the state budget being responsible for establishing new enterprises or giving financial assistance to those whose development was indispensable. Wages are based on productivity, and are thus variable from one firm to another, and there is a fund which, in proportion to the increase of profits, pays bonuses to the work-force and the managers for the fulfilment of plans. Hence enterprises have considerable freedom in the use of their financial resources, but it is the state which fixes prices for a five-year period.

Hungary has followed this example in part. But it is in Poland that business enterprises have greater autonomy than in any other eastern country. Their production and supply plans are based on contracts drawn up among themselves; each is consulted about the fixing of prices and the distribution of investments and other funds; there is no longer state control over materials and the progress of production. At the beginning of 1956, workers' councils were organized; but this step towards self-management functioned badly as a result of conflicts between the workers and the executives. Often the workers could not understand the point of long-term forecasts, nor that it was in the enterprise's interest to fulfil them. In the end the experiment seems to have come to nothing, and it disappeared in 1960.

Another common characteristic of all the east European countries – apart from the large place reserved in cities for buildings of collective use – is the low cost of services. Transport is very cheap, almost free; in Czechoslovakia, for example, it is five to six times lower than in France. In Hungary and Rumania, trams and telephone calls cost the equivalent of 2 British pennies or USA cents. Homes and apartments are particularly cheap: in East Germany and Hungary they cost about £6 or $14.50 a month per family; in Czechoslovakia two rooms can be rented for £4 or $9.50 a month. In all eastern countries the share of social services in the budget is very considerable. In Czechoslovakia items such as housing, health and education absorb 28·1 per cent of the total national income. Every employee enjoys a month's paid holiday for eleven months' work in the same firm. In Poland the annual vacation is thirty days. Medical services are free in all the People's Democracies without exception. Large families benefit from family allowances and reduced fares. In Bulgaria pharmaceutical products are exceedingly cheap. Even tiny Albania, where there were only 8 hospitals in 1938, had 19 in 1966 with 4,000 beds, 96 lying-in homes, 450 dispensaries. There are many day-nurseries and kinder-gartens which can also be used on week-ends.

In all these countries, where the proportion of illiterates (except in Czechoslovakia and East Germany) was considerable, and where only the children of the upper bourgeoisie and the aristocracy received a western education, the essential drive has been to make up as quickly as possible for lost time. Education at all levels has been expanded. Even more than in the west, it has taken on a mass character. It is free at all levels and is no longer restricted to the development of an élite. Minorities, such as the Hungarians, Germans and Jews in Rumania, and even the 4,000 Lusatian Sorbs in East Germany, are taught in their national languages. Education in science, mathematics, physics and technology is particularly developed in order to create specialized workers and administrators to carry through industrialization. In all these countries, education is non-parochial, obligatory, democratic and Marxist-oriented. It has rapidly absorbed the great mass of illiter-ates, of whom there remain only a few among the older generations.

The education of women, in these countries where work is obli-gatory for all, has expanded along with that of men. In Poland the number of children at school rose from 1,700,000 in 1958 to 3,760,000 in 1964, and there is a growing number in higher education, as in the mixed technical and agricultural colleges. The number of pupils in primary and secondary schools in Albania rose from 30,000 to 190,000 in 1966, and the University of Tirana had an enrolment of 1,600. In Bulgaria, where there is a system that links primary and secondary education in an eleven-year cycle, the school-leaving age was raised to 16 years in 1966–67. This is the first country in the world in terms of numbers of students: candidates for higher education are so numerous (five to ten candidates for each place) that they are subjected to a severe university entrance examination, but even so there is a glut of doctors and engineers; the number of doctors is so much in excess of the country's needs that they are 'exported' to Africa and even to Sweden.

During recent years, production has been diversified and de-centralized, and the stress is on quality rather than on quantity, which previously was the essential objective. This change took place under the influence of theories propounded by the great Soviet economists (among whom Libermann is the best known) and those of Poland, some of whom (Lange, Kalecki, Lipinski) have a world reputation. The greater autonomy allowed to business enterprises has had a favourable effect on production in all respects, while relations with the west – commercial agreements, tourism, more freedom to travel abroad (which is complete in Poland) – facilitate improvements in living conditions and encourage the desire to attain western standards of comfort and recreation.

Working conditions have improved. In Poland the unions nominate the heads of businesses, who have a right of veto over the decisions of the state economic planning executives. A bonus-system of profit participation has been started. This can reach up to 80 per cent of annual wages, and 50 per cent for the heads of departments and engineers; if, however, the firm has poor results, the salaries may be cut by up to 25 per cent, though the wages of ordinary workers remain fixed.

Differences between currencies and their frequent inconvertibility make it difficult to compare wages and standards of living. At most, one can compare purchasing-power in terms of certain foods or manufactured products. We have seen that lodgings, health services and transportation are either free or extremely cheap; on the other hand, clothing (not very elegant and often of poor quality) and shoes are expensive. Imported goods, especially luxuries, are either impossible to find or exceedingly dear. On the whole, though much improved (particularly in recent years), the standard of living in the People's Democracies remains lower than that of the western countries, but no one has to go without essentials. Criticisms are directed principally against the poor quality of services and goods, delays and difficulties in distribution, and the frequency and discomfort of long queues at shop-doors.

Albania remains apart; it is still almost entirely agricultural, its pro-Chinese political orientation has caused almost total isolation, and it has only a few industries (breweries, sugar and olive-oil refineries). But the other People's Democracies appear to have achieved considerable progress, accelerated by the more or less advanced measures of liberalization introduced in recent years. In Hungary there is a wide choice of food products, many of them foreign. Food-shops in Poland are well stocked; the number of automobiles has increased; the countryside shows signs of catching up with the cities; there is work for all (and also much wastage of labour); and, as in Bulgaria and East Germany, there are many opportunities for doctors, engineers, and qualified technicians. Probably Czechoslovakia has the highest standard of living among the countries of the eastern bloc, in spite of the need to import a great deal of food and manufactured products. But in all there is now a decent standard of living; only in Albania are there still underfed people.

In addition, the style of living shows signs of change, at least in the more developed countries. In 1950 a survey was taken of 1,000 Czechoslovak families living in new housing estates in order to ascertain the wishes of the population. It revealed a general desire to make better use of collective facilities (supermarkets, collective food-shops, self-service restaurants, etc.) so as to increase the amount of time devoted to leisure and culture. Of those questioned, 71 per cent were in favour of meals outside the home, 75 per cent for laundromats and pressing facilities, 60 per cent wanted equipment provided for clothing repairs and sewing, and 50 per cent were for development of green areas and shopping centres within the housing complex. They asked for an increase in the number of rooms (one for each member of the family) and a larger living room. The current pattern envisages an apartment of three rooms, kitchen, bathroom, wall cupboards, food-cabinet, storeroom, with laundry, drying and pressing facilities in the building. This type of construction has been started in the coal-mining and metallurgical centres where there is shift-work (Kladno-Rozdelov, Pardubice-Dukla, Gottwaldow, Bratislava, as well as several districts in Prague).

It is in the sphere of housing that the situation in eastern Europe is least good. Though building is under the direction of town-planners who are generally innovators, it is far from being completed: East Berlin is still a vast construction-area. The apartments are often too small and are occupied by several families, but the low rents mitigate the discontent which this causes.

The rupture with the Soviet Union and Comecon placed Yugoslavia in a difficult position, forcing it to embark on the so-called 'Yugoslav experiment' and to establish its Socialism on new foundations. The range of wages has been expanded; the lowest have been raised. Whereas ten years ago a family spent more than half of its income on food, now the percentage has fallen to 37 per cent. One family in ten possesses an automobile, and hire-purchase of furniture, vacuum cleaners, television sets, etc., has become possible.

80 Scrap-metal sculpture in Poland   81 The city centre of Eisenhütte, East Germany

82 A supermarket in Warsaw

131

As in all the People's Democracies, medical care and hospital treatment are free in Yugoslavia, and the sick receive an allowance of at least 80 – sometimes 100 – per cent of their wages. Retirement is at the age of 55 for men with 35 years of service, and at the age of 50 and 30 years of service for women. Agricultural workers and private craftsmen also receive social security benefits.

There has been a considerable effort to develop education. Since 1958, educational establishments have been autonomous, managed by a collective composed of teaching personnel, citizens elected by the directors, and delegates of social organizations. The number of pupils has increased tenfold since 1940. Secondary school students elect their own representatives to the administrative councils.

Craftsmen and small shopkeepers still exist: tailors, hairdressers, shoe-shops, butchers, taxi-drivers, proprietors of small hotels, restaurants and cafés. Fruit and vegetables are abundant in the markets. The private sector tends to grow, always under the proviso that there shall be no exploitation of human labour. Many shops do a brisk business with luxury goods from the west; one sees men's clothes in French, British or Italian ready-made styles. The reconstruction of cities has made possible a relative degree of comfort in housing.

From the intellectual point of view, the party's ideological monopoly no longer exists. Although it is still a one-party government, there is freedom within the party, and opposition may be expressed within the party so long as it does not attack the bases of the regime. Proceedings have been taken, however, against Professor Mihajlo Mihajlov, who demanded a democracy of the western type, and Milovan Djilas, one of the founders of the regime. In general, however, there are no longer any great difficulties in entering or leaving the country. Scientific and artistic activity (with a vogue for abstract painting) is free, but the only purchasers can be the official organs, and they show little appreciation of contemporary works. There are two universities, a 'popular university', intended mainly for townsfolk and peasants, and a 'workers' university', with twenty-five branches, intended for working people, recruited by the unions and workers' councils, who study economic and social subjects.

Western influence is also evident: along with traditional songs and folk dances, there is appreciation of the western theatre, pop music and modern literature. Djilas, who was expelled from the party in 1954 for having written *The New Class*, in which he inveighed against the reappearance of a ruling class enjoying social privileges and economic advantages, seems to have exaggerated. Though highly placed members of the administration, whom Tito himself denounced and opposed, may have lived in luxury, they could not constitute a class apart – any more than in the USSR – since it was impossible for them to convert their income into capital. But it cannot be denied that in Yugoslavia – as indeed in the west – the industrial civilization in the process of formation favours the managerial class as well as a proliferating bureaucracy. And the latter is more important here than in many other countries, because the federal character of the state increases the number of both the central and the local organs of government.

Yugoslavia today can be classed in the category of 'moderately developed countries' – but at the bottom of the list. It maintains economic relations with the Common Market countries, with Comecon and with EFTA. It has recently concluded a contract with an American company; for the first time, American capitalism will thus be able to penetrate a Communist state.

The 'new Socialism' created by the Yugoslav experiment is a source of great interest and attraction to a number of European

83 A state shop in Belgrade

Socialists who reject the Soviet model and seek their own path to Socialism. Yugoslavia enjoys a real internal stability and its liberalization is more advanced than that of any other eastern country. It is having, however, some difficulty in reconciling self-management and state intervention – the latter indispensable to a Socialist economy in the making – with the liberalization of external commerce which is necessary if the country wants to develop trade with the capitalist countries. Another impediment is the differences of level which exist among the component republics of the federal state. Yugoslavia is a federation of six republics (Serbia, Slovenia, Croatia, Bosnia-Herzegovina, Montenegro, Macedonia) and two autonomous territories (Voivodin and Kosmet); it is also a collection of peoples professing three religions (Orthodox, Catholic, Muslim), speaking three different languages (Serbo-Croatian, Macedonian and Albanian) and using two alphabets (Cyrillic and Latin). Western customs and the western style of life mix with those of the orient, but only the Albanian and Macedonian minorities seem to show centrifugal tendencies.

In the course of this brief description of the society of the two Europes, with such different structures, we have tried to show that, in spite of rapid economic progress, the eastern countries, for the various reasons we have indicated, do not yet enjoy the same standard of living as those of the west. Their social legislation is extremely generous and, in contrast to the situation of barely twenty-five years ago, no one any longer suffers from hunger. At present a somewhat timid process of liberalization is taking place in their economic as well as in their social organization, and this will allow them to reduce progressively the differences that still exist. It may be halted and it may be reversed; but the imperatives of industrial society, into which the whole continent has entered, will force them along this path.

IV INTELLECTUAL AND CULTURAL LIFE

Communications facilities of all sorts; the proliferation of libraries, exhibitions, art galleries, concerts, music festivals; the international character of the important churches: these are the factors which, since the end of the war, have made exchanges possible and played a part in endowing our contemporary world with that standardization which is one of its principal characteristics. Though the multiplicity of languages favours the differentiation of various literatures, and historical traditions encourage national schools in the arts, at least in the sphere of science one can call uniformity complete. The only differences that exist are due to the inequality of scientific equipment, itself a function of the wealth of each country and the level of its education.

As a result of the great increase in specialized research institutes (even in countries of lesser political significance, such as Belgium, Switzerland and Scandinavia), the expansion of universities and the upsurge of the student population, the great number of scientific reviews, as well as the congresses which bring scientists together and facilitate the exchange of ideas, discoveries can no longer be the achievement of a single researcher but must be considered as a collective task in which the scientists of all countries participate. The interest of governments in scientific research has also contributed to its internationalization. The USA and the USSR have possibilities of research and discovery with which no country of western Europe, once 'the centre of modern science', can any longer compete. In both of the super-powers there is an abundance of financial and material resources; their governments and private institutions with generous endowments encourage research; and the USA has the added advantage of being able to attract many European scientists. It is just possible that this will be equalized one day by such organizations as the Centre for Nuclear Study and Research (Euratom) and the European Organization of Space Research. In any case, the links of cooperation or dependence between all countries are such that it is no longer possible to distinguish among scientific advances those which are the product of 'European science' alone.

The two uninterrupted crises of Fascism and global war could not fail to affect the ideas and works of artists and writers. The most brilliant and innovative centre of intellectual and artistic life in the world, Europe found itself after 1933 in a calamitous situation. From that date, the great intellectual, scientific and artistic *milieux* of Germany began to erode. Racial persecution and the rigours of a blind and ignorant censorship led a great many writers, scientists and artists to seek refuge in foreign countries. Some of those who remained kept quiet or passed over to the resistance (e.g., Ernst Jünger and Reinhold Schneider); very few served the regime. The emigration had two results: one, paradoxically, was the diffusion of German intellectual influence in countries where it had barely existed before; and the other was to deprive Germany of scientists whose work contributed to the Allied victory.

After 1939, Poland, the USSR and the other eastern countries occupied by the German army were subjected to a systematic massacre of their élites; we know that Hitler intended to reduce their populations to virtual slavery (to work on the land and labour in the service of the master race). The west was relatively (and temporarily) spared, but it was subjected to very tight censorship, numerous arrests, destruction of 'Marxist' works and prohibition of their reprint or sale (the Otto list in France). Nevertheless, a reduced intellectual life was maintained: in Poland there were what amounted to clandestine universities. Many intellectuals joined the emigrants of other occupied countries overseas; everywhere opposition newspapers, pamphlets and books were published, either disguised (*Les Mouches* by Jean-Paul Sartre) or under pseudonyms (in France, for example, the booklets of Mauriac, Aragon and Vercors, who was the clandestine publisher of *Editions de Minuit*). For its part, the French National Committee of Authors distributed its pamphlets *sub rosa*, and everyone made ready to take up the struggle in the open after the liberation.

From 1944–45, when liberty was restored, works published abroad began to arrive in Europe. Europe's intellectuals made contact again with foreign ideas, and there was a surge of intense creative activity. It was a real resurrection, limited only by the scarcity of paper. All trends of thought were expressed and older ones prolonged their existence; but numerous and fruitful innovations appeared, which distinguished the new works from the old, except in countries remaining under dictatorial regimes: Spain, Portugal and the USSR.

Matter and form were transformed under the impact of the nightmare that had just ended.

All the creative manifestations of the intellect were thus renewed. Since the end of the nineteenth century, the great discoveries of mathematicians and physicists had created a new physics which completely overturned traditional scientific conceptions about the universe and, consequently, about man. It was inevitable that these influences should be felt in other spheres of intellectual life. Painting was the first of the arts to take new directions, then literature, sculpture and architecture followed; the cinema, though producing occasional masterpieces, did not manage to find a balance. Even more than in the preceding centuries, innovations, sometimes rash and disconcerting to the public, existed side by side with an art and literature conforming to traditional models.

Once Freud's work became well-known, a large area of investigation opened up to writers (in fact, the surrealists had already explored it) through psychoanalysis, which seeks to uncover the deep sources of man's behaviour by interpreting his dreams. This study reinforced the reaction against rationalism. Classical psychology and realism, which was content to describe and explain the world, gave way to imagination, whose creative power was exalted and whose manifestations, even among the insane and those under the influence of drugs, were of interest. The same division between traditional literary works and a revolutionary literature is evident in the theatre and the cinema, as well as in the plastic arts.

In the years following the end of operations, literature was 'engaged'; it preached a new ideal, that of the resistance, criticizing the institutions considered responsible for the carnage and the regimes which started it. But the resumption of relations with the USA and the sensational discoveries resulting from the splitting of the atom and from astronautics, rapidly opened up unlimited perspectives (at the same time that the panic fear of atomic warfare awoke). There was an enlargement of horizons that made it possible to envisage a liberation of the individual, as well as conditions of life that were completely new, completely different from those before the war. The new horizon was planetary, wide open to all the speculations of the spirit; henceforward, the world was a unity which breaks through all frontiers, and man's potentialities appeared limitless.

A large body of resistance literature, notably in France, Italy, Norway and Greece, praised the heroes in the struggle against the occupation forces. Nevertheless, these works, except for those of Marxist inspiration, were far from being optimistic. Among the different currents, the Marxist one was strongest at the beginning. It owed its success to the prestige of the victories won by the Soviet Army and to a social system which exercised a real attraction on many intellectuals eager for renewal and social justice. Powerful in 1944–47, this current weakened under the effect of rapid improvement in the standard of living, the impression made by the Berlin blockade, the rupture between the wartime Allies which gave rise to the Cold War, and the Korean War which threatened to spark off a new global war. Besides, the rigidity of the Soviet model – until Stalin's death – wrecked the attempts of certain Communists (such as the Italian followers of Antonio Gramsci, a victim of Fascism) to remodel Marxism. Finally there was a desire to see each Communist Party free to choose its own path to Communism. The endeavours of Togliatti, head of the Italian Communist Party, and of French philosophers such as Althusser and Garaudy, failed to preserve its earlier importance for Communism, which was gradually abandoned by a considerable portion of the European intelligentsia. The preponderant current, with many variants, is that of atheistic humanism, essentially characterized by a sense of the absurdity of life.

The intellectual life of defeated Germany remained for several years outside the main stream of the European renaissance. Under the knockout blow of the collapse of the Third Reich, its material ruin and the Allied occupation, Germany's situation appeared hopeless. Plunged into a kind of intellectual night, it discovered the crimes of Nazism slowly and tardily, tried to understand what had happened, and analyzed Germany's position and that of the world around it. It took a number of years for German intellectuals to attain full consciousness of the extent of the disaster and the true character of the demolished regime: the concentration camps, Hitler's desire for the systematic and methodical destruction of whole peoples. In 1945, whatever might be the prestige and authority of the survivors of the preceding epoch (e.g., Thomas and Heinrich Mann, Franz Werfel), it was other writers, such as Theodor Plivier, Karl Jaspers and Alfred Döblin, who distinguished themselves in their critical description of the death camps, the extermination of the Jews, the sufferings of displaced persons and bombing victims, the distress of combatants on the Eastern Front, and the chaos of the defeated armies. In 1947 a group of talented writers of all leanings, based in Munich, joined forces and called themselves Group 47. In their novels and plays they expressed without restraint what the Nazi years had been like. They showed where the responsibility lay and argued that the entire German people must share it. In its pessimism, Group 47 participated in the general tendency of western literature to denounce the nationalism of the preceding age, the injustices of the social structure, the humiliation of man in modern society. All the German writers (the most important in West Germany are at present Günter Grass, Heinrich Böll and Uwe Johnson) are concerned with the absurdity of bourgeois pretensions and the hypocrisy of 'the German miracle'. The theatre, so important in both Germanies, has developed the same ideas under the influence of Bertolt Brecht and his principal disciples, Helmut Baierl and Peter Weiss. In spite of the police and the Berlin Wall, the two Germanies have close intellectual relations.

In France the great writers of the inter-war years – André Malraux, François Mauriac, Julien Green, Roger Martin du Gard and Henry de Montherlant – have abandoned the novel; dead writers, such as Paul Valéry, Jean Giraudoux, André Gide and Antoine de Saint-Exupéry, have been relatively forsaken; the Communist Louis Aragon returned to pure poetry and wrote a historical novel. In fact the literature that found most favour with a public disappointed in the conventional variety was that of the liberation, whose most impressive representatives and interpreters were Albert Camus, Jean-Paul Sartre, Simone de Beauvoir and Maurice Merleau-Ponty. It was these philosophers and writers who, inspired by the ideas of Heidegger, Jaspers and Husserl, made existentialism fashionable. Their works offered the pessimistic picture of an artificial, absurd, incomprehensible and useless world, in which man feels frustrated and cheated, for 'it is a suspended death' and 'every society creates its own hell'. Under cover of this catastrophic concept of the world, literature has been invaded by sexuality, sadism, and at the same time a certain type of escapism – represented, for example, by Julien Gracq and by André Pieyre de Mandiargue's studies of the fantastic and bizarre.

It is the theatre – the collective art *par excellence* – which best expresses this view of the world. There has even emerged a 'theatre of provocation', not so much in the plays of Jean Anouilh as in those of Sartre and especially of Jean Genet, Samuel Beckett, Arthur Adamov and Eugène Ionesco, who exploit the most scabrous and sordid subjects, and seek to shock the public. They represent what has been called anti-theatre, substituting condemnation of the Algerian war and virulent criticism of social injustice and inequality for the former psychological concept of theatre.

While Christian literature also has felt the influence of existentialism (e.g., Gabriel Marcel), it is represented above all by Georges Bernanos (*The Dialogue of Carmelites*, with its theme that 'living degrades') and the personalism of Emmanuel Mounier, editor of the review *Esprit*. But most of its writers are little known, except for Paul Claudel (in fact a pre-war figure) and Pierre Teilhard de Chardin, no doubt better known by name than read, whose ambiguous and vague thinking aims at a global vision of the world, its origins and its destiny.

Since the 1950s, the influence of the 'engaged' generation has begun to recede. Taste has shifted to various kinds of escapist literature: science fiction, travel books, more or less fictional reporting, historical novels.

But most of all it is the 'new novel' which, though it, too, is pessimistic, appears to be replacing the novel of the absurd, described by Pierre de Boisdeffre as 'that monotonous act of accusation against man, nature and society'. The so-called new novel, whose leading light is Michel Butor, is not 'engaged'; discarding the basic concepts of the psychological novel, it simply describes a man's acts impartially, without attempting to give them a psychological interpretation or to understand anything about his past or present condition. Thus the novel becomes limited to a minute account of the thousand details of everyday life which appear to be of little interest. This is an impersonal and unimaginative literature; Alain Robbe-Grillet claims to have 'assassinated the object'.

More recently, the tendency seems to be towards a return to psychological analysis, reflecting a total nihilism. Generally speaking, the principal writers of our times are not concerned with portraying and explaining the world, but with striking at its roots. 'The absurd,' writes Boisdeffre, 'has replaced providence.' A literature of decadence? The phrase is exaggerated; and yet there can be little doubt that the preceding generation had achievements to its credit of higher quality than the present one, and that works which end up abolishing not only the subject but the language itself (such as Samuel Beckett's *Molloy*), and which are obsessed with death and the inanity of human life, must logically lead to the destruction of literature itself.

Italy, too, on the morrow of the liberation, experienced a brilliant neo-realistic renaissance, with writers of great talent who devoted themselves to criticism of the society bred by Fascism, its corrupt ruling class and their hypocrisy: Alberto Moravia, Cesare Pavese, Carlo Levi, Elio Vittorini, Italo Calvino, Danilo Dolci, Pier Paolo Pasolini – to say nothing of the lively plays of Ugo Betti and Diego Fabri.

British writers, more strongly influenced than the French by American novels, were also affected by the works of Joyce and Kafka. Here, too, alongside a literature of traditional style, a whole group of 'angry young men' – Kingsley Amis, Colin Wilson, John Wain, Alan Sillitoe, among others – dissected the great social problems with humour and in a spirit critical of the Establishment. A brilliant theatre of protest also emerged, distinguished by the work of John Osborne, Arnold Wesker and Joan Littlewood. Their plays had a systematic vulgarity which stressed the frustrations felt by the post-war generation; they were in some ways the mouthpiece of social misfits, drop-outs and rebels.

Spain's intellectual élite – as in Nazi Germany – was decimated during the Civil War or forced to emigrate to France or South America. Yet, in spite of strict censorship and intense religious intolerance, there is a school of young avant-garde Spanish writers, all of whom were children at the time of the Civil War. In the neo-realistic tradition, they barely disguise their hidden frustrations and their criticism of the regime. Their works are naturally published abroad – mainly in France; they include Camilo José Cela and Ana Maria Matute (the two most important novelists), Juan Goytisolo and Miguel Delibes.

Soviet writers have been grouped, since before 1941, in a single organization, once headed by Gorki, which adopted the principle that 'there is no place for a neutral art in a classless society'. Their outlook is expressed in 'socialist realism', which considers dialectical materialism both as a *Weltanschauung* and as the source of artistic creation. From 1935, in anticipation of the threatening war, patriotic literature became increasingly important; it praised the heroes of the past – as in the works of Ilya Ehrenburg and Mikhail Aleksandrovich Sokolov, who finished his novel *And Quiet Flows the Don* in 1940. Once the German onslaught began, Soviet writers devoted their talents to war themes. But following the war they were subjected to the influence of A. A. Zhdanov, whose devastating intellectual dictator-

84 *The Chairs*, by Eugène Ionesco

ship, even after his disappearance in 1948, stifled talent under the pretext of combating 'ideological errors' and cosmopolitanism, i.e. the influence of foreign literature representing the 'corrupt west'. Writers were harassed and censured; the main permissible themes were the reconstruction of the country, the patriotic war, the necessity to resist bourgeois culture. The works written in this period are too often edifying, moralistic and boring. After Stalin's death there was a change: socialist realism is still the rule, but there is somewhat greater liberty of expression, and an opposition has appeared that is critical of the regime. The best known of the newer critical writers are Aleksander Solzhenitsyn and the poet Yevgey Yevtushenko. At the same time there has been an interesting revival of peasant literature. The greater part of the works that are published are novels or short stories of rural life. Sometimes they criticize agricultural policy and point out its mistakes; in the main, however, they concentrate on life in the *kolkhoz* and its individual dramas, giving a candid and engaging picture of peasant life. This peasant literature, which emerged around 1953, was revived by reflection on moral problems, the sense of life, and the hardships of the Soviet peasant.

85 *Les Paravents,*
by Jean Genet

86 *Look Back in Anger,*
by John Osborne

87 *Waiting for Godot,*
by Samuel Beckett

The People's Democracies have followed a similar development, taking into account their national traditions. During the war and after, principally in Yugoslavia and Poland, the literature of the *maquis* predominated; this was mixed with the socialist realism imposed during the Zhdanov period, except for Poland, where it did not take hold until after 1950, and Yugoslavia, where emancipation began several years after the break with the USSR and writers turned towards the west for their models. The prevalence of socialist realism in Polish writing has led to the decline of a narrow nationalist particularism. This is true also of Hungary, which has writers of European reputation, such as Paul Szabo, Louis Nagy and the surrealist Tibor Dery. As for Rumania, its best known writers have emigrated to the west: Mircea Eliade and Eugène Ionesco, who now write in English or French.

The war accelerated the decline of Paris as the principal art centre; London, and particularly New York, have become the great art markets, as well as Zurich, Milan, Düsseldorf and Cassel. Paris used to be not only the city where the principal artists worked, where the great movements and world careers began, but it was also the principal market for works of art. Today, outside of Paris, there are galleries of wide reputation whose exhibitions attract art-lovers from all over the world. As a result, artistic work has more than ever assumed an international character; this reduces the distinctions among national schools, which used to be more clearly defined. The reasons for this are both the emergence of a school of talented American painters, and the emigration of a great number of artists who were threatened by the German invasion because they represented the 'degenerate art' that Hitler detested. In a general way, art shows the same uneasiness as literature, science and music; it is felt that truth is only an appearance since it is relative, and that the work of art must be metaphysically inspired and not representative. There is a complete break with the past: artists no longer aspire to represent and explain reality, but to create it.

The new generation of artists born during the war have an extremely fertile boldness. This is well expressed by Bernard Dorival: 'What the 1914 war did to the Impressionists – disdained in 1913, classics in 1919 – the 1939 war accomplished for Bonnard, Rouault, Matisse, Braque, Picasso, Léger, Dufy, Villon. Their work was already the subject of discussion just as the war started; suddenly in 1945 they stood out at a distance and the effect was to reveal their true dimensions, the dimensions of giants, so majestic and so authentic that nothing could ever again cast doubt upon their contribution. . . . The younger generation have no intention of discarding it since, courageous, daring, revolutionary, it corresponds to their aspirations and to the needs of the hour . . . it seems the only possible path for young French painters'; their 'spiritual fathers are Bonnard and Cézanne, whose work, formed of disparate elements, they are completing.'

In 1945 the art movement erupted. Some remained figurative painters, among them Communists such as Fougeron, Taslitzky, Venitien, and in Italy Renato Guttuso, who rallied to the socialist realism school. The rest, divided into two groups, expressed themselves in two different languages: that of neo-realism and that of neo-

88 *Danse Brune*, by Jean Dubuffet (1959)   89 *Composition in Red and Yellow*, by Poliakoff (1954)

expressionism (e.g. Tal Coat). The one is the 'art actuel' of Bernard Lorjou, Bernard Buffet, Gruber, Claude Venard, a group that were also called 'l'homme témoin' in 1948. This is an 'engaged' art, inspired by everyday reality and loosely related to socialist realism, which aims at painting 'the living man, with his joys or sufferings, his pride, his reflexes, his feelings, his muscles'. The other group is that of the abstract painters – the 'art of today', which has been strongly influenced by the American, Jackson Pollock. Rejected since 1947 by the socialist realists, and categorized as 'tachism' by certain critics, the school has been defined by Pierre Soulages in this way: 'Painting must be called abstract when one can recognize in it nothing of the objective reality that constitutes the normal medium of our life. . . . An abstract work is one in which no suggestion of an image is voluntarily accepted.' It is a 'modified cubism' transformed into 'informal painting'; by granting unlimited freedom for each individual, it rejects composition and plastic refinement, and 'seeks to give every opening to the total anarchy of the real'. This is a sober art, sometimes only

146

90 *Fort d'Antibes*, by Nicolas de Staël ▶

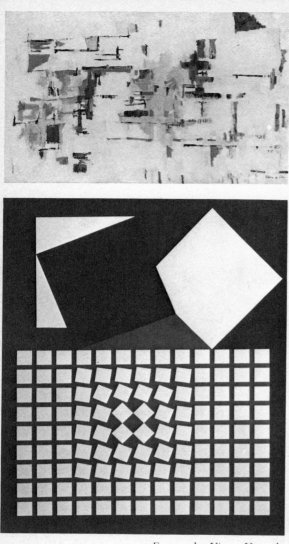

91 *Painting*, by Maria Helena Vieira da Silva (1953)

93 *T 54–16*, by Hans Hartung

92 *100 F. 1957*, by Victor Vasarely

94 *23 mai 1953*, by Pierre Soulages

black and white. Among its representatives are Hans Hartung, Serge Poliakoff, Nicolas de Staël, Raoul Ubac, Gérard Schneider, Maria Helena Vieira da Silva, Zao Wouki and William Scott. Their work shows that abstract art is capable of as many varieties as figurative painting, and certain abstract painters do not despise perspective, modelling, chiaroscuro, and other traditional painting devices.

A new form of figurative art, which came from the United States under the patronage of Marcel Duchamp, was dubbed 'Pop art' by an English critic. These artists take their themes directly from commercial art, from 'comics' and strip cartoons, from objects in everyday use (such as Duchamp's defiant juxtaposition of a urinal and a soup-tureen). Pop art has found much sympathy in Great Britain, as in the work of David Hockney and Richard Hamilton, but far less on the Continent. It has proliferated into numerous other movements, most of which seek at present to break down the boundaries between painting, sculpture, furniture and actuality (assemblages, happenings, etc.).

Things are very different in the USSR and the People's Democracies. Here socialist realism, linked to Communist ideology, has emerged victorious. We are not very familiar with this realistic, resolutely materialist art; all we know is that there are very lively centres of activity which borrow their themes from history, folklore, the details of the daily life of workers and peasants. There are also regional schools in the various republics of the USSR, notably in Georgia. Criticism is directed against anyone who might be tempted

95 Still-life with Chip-Fryer, by John Bratby (1954)

96 Just What Is It that Makes Today's Homes so Different, so Appealing?, collage by Richard Hamilton (1956)

to imitate the 'formalists' Picasso and Matisse. Yet internal voices are increasingly raised against the official art of the eastern countries for being excessively academic and conventional.

SCULPTURE

Like painting, sculpture has gone through significant mutations, though the traditional means of expression endured for a long time. Long after painters had committed themselves to change, sculptors were unwilling to abandon the foundations of their art. All too often their attempts at 'modernity' were superficial and conventional. Nevertheless, important innovations occurred as a result of the search for new solutions to the basic problems of contemporary sculpture: the choice of materials, space and movement. In Great Britain, Anthony Caro began working with plaster, beams and metal plate, and his pupils at the St Martin's School of Art in London followed his example by using glass fibre and plastic. Other sculptors used fabrics and painted paper pasted together.

The works produced have been diverse and rich. Eduardo Chillida makes delicate objects of welded iron; César first mixes iron and plaster, then repoussé lead-sheet and iron-wire which he solders, twists and distends; Fritz Wotruba, on the other hand, retains a monumental concept by polishing and refining a block of stone with projections or depressions or slight curves. Other sculptors immerse mineral slag or coal in cement, or the artist may model the most unusual objects out of metal waste, rusted bolts, scrap-iron, even the remains of a burnt automobile, conforming to the maxim that 'art brut' (raw art) emerges directly out of the material. Among the younger artists, the 1960s developed a ferment of experimentation: experiments with light and water, plastic facsimiles of real people, combinations of painting and sculpture, whole environments. The most famous forerunners of the young experimenters were Giacometti and Brancusi.

The number of art-lovers has grown prodigiously. They are either disinterested, desiring only to satisfy their aesthetic taste, or they are seeking profitable investments in 'sure values'. Thus the material success of many artists is real, but it is a function of the prosperity of the European (and American) economy. This commercial aspect of the works of certain artists may have a regrettable influence on their independence. No contemporary artist, not even the most eminent,

·99 *Grandi contatti*,
bronze by
Gio Pomodoro (1962) ▶

97 *Piazza*, bronze by
Alberto Giacometti (1948)

98 *Reclining figure*,
bronze by
Fritz Wotruba (1960)

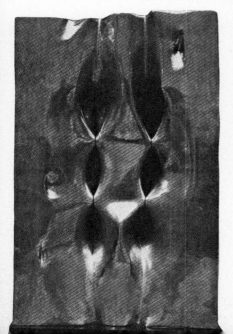

100 *Dream Anvil*, by
Eduardo Chillida
(1962)

can be compared to the great masters of the past. Most art critics agree that, in spite of the remarkable revival of the plastic arts since the Second World War, no real geniuses have been brought to light.

In the sphere of music, too, a profound revolution has taken place with the diffusion of the twelve-tone scale, although it has not completely dethroned the more traditional music of composers like Darius Milhaud, Georges Auric, Paul Hindemith and their successors. During the inter-war period, the school of Vienna – Arnold Schoenberg and his pupils Alban Berg and Anton Webern – had already used the twelve-tone system and atonality, which had very little relation to classical music. Theirs was a music in which a mathematical logic ruled the composition. Since 1945 its representatives have been Olivier Messaien, Pierre Boulez and René Leibowitz. This *musique concrète* has become established in France, West Germany (Hans Werner Henze), Scandinavia (Hilding Rosenberg and Bo Nilsson), Italy (Luigi Dallapiccola and his disciples) and Great Britain (Richard Rodney Bennett and Malcolm Williamson).

Many of these composers also adopt electronic devices for the production of non-musical sound: Pierre Schaeffer is a well-known example, and the German Stockhausen fuses the two techniques in a complementary way. The execution of these works is so difficult that only few orchestras are capable of performing them; their diffusion is slow, because audiences need a long period to appreciate them.

Closely linked with *musique concrète*, the art of dance has been revolutionized by Maurice Béjart and his Ballet of the Twentieth Century. In 1959 he produced his *Ninth Symphony*, then he created *Symphony for a Single Man*, followed by some fifty more ballets. His principle is to make what he creates topical, to express the present. (His *Temptation of St Anthony* shows the similarities between the fall of the Roman Empire and the present epoch.) For him, the dance is a 'juxtaposition of arts'; he seeks a synthesis of folklore elements, new elements of sound, especially voices. His successes have been considerable and his influence is growing. In the USSR, which remains a nursery of exceptional dancers, academic ballet continues its exclusive reign.

101 The Béjart Ballet Company

Both an art and an industry, the cinema has passed through several crises in the last twenty-five years, and has only rarely found the formula which reconciles the two conditions on which its existence depends: the rising costs of production, which demands large capital, and artistic quality. The result is that increasingly the commercial film, made solely for profit, tends to become the rule. Hence there is a very clear decline in quality – to which television contributes – and a reduced number of cinema audiences. Moreover, being the only form of art that reaches the masses, the cinema is a powerful means of conditioning crowds, and is used for this purpose by governments (all of which exercise censorship of some sort) and financial groups whose cooperation is essential to it. And the growing vogue for war films, crime and espionage films, the scenes of violence they show and their increasing emphasis on sex all have a strong influence on the minds of youth.

The main effect of the Second World War was to condemn each national cinema to isolation, to cut it off from foreign productions and to reduce its material means of production (shortages of film, studios, electricity). In this way the war was responsible for the birth of a national cinema in countries which had not been film-producers

153

before: Yugoslavia, Hungary, Switzerland, Norway, Czechoslovakia. Immediately after communications were re-established following the war, there was an invasion of American films, some of which had been made by European émigrés. New and experimental American inventions became general: the triple-screen, stereophonic sound, cinemascope. European audiences also became aware for the first time of Japanese, Indian and Mexican films.

The film-makers of European countries quickly resumed their activities. The triumph of Italian neo-realism, a brilliant manifestation of the post-war cinema renaissance, led to the disappearance of literary and theatrical conventions. The numerous war and Resistance films gave way to the more individual works of outstanding directors, and occasional films of great beauty, such as David Lean's *Brief Encounter*. The renaissance in British film-making occasionally escaped from the commercial formula around 1960 (*Room at the Top*, *Saturday Night and Sunday Morning*), but this was short-lived. The French cinema revived at that time, especially as the older generation was overtaken by the 'new wave', producing a complete victory of amorality in the works of Roger Vadim (and his star, Brigitte Bardot), Louis Malle, Jean-Luc Godard, François Truffaut, Claude Chabrol and Alain Resnais. The Spanish cinema revealed the work of Juan Antonio Bardem, and in Sweden Ingmar Bergman proved to be a world master.

The crisis in the American film industry also caused changes. After having attracted the best European artists and technicians to Hollywood, American producers began to make their films more cheaply in Europe itself. In 1960, under the impact of television's direct methods, there was another shift, to *film vérité* and the British 'free cinema', which aims to be a copy of real life and often uses non-professional actors, as had been the case in the post-war Italian films (*Bicycle Thieves*). This type of cinema seeks to be a mere witness; but sincerity is often lacking, except in such unusual cases as Agnès Varda's *Cléo de 5 à 7*. Sometimes the action unfolds without prior construction (e.g., Antonioni's *L'Avventura*), or it may be the memories, thoughts and imaginations of people which determine the development of the dramatic theme. We seem to be moving towards a new form of cinema – what Pierre Leprohon calls 'the cinema novel'.

103 *Pigsty*, directed by Pasolini

105 *Shame*, directed by Ingmar Bergman

107 *Saturday Night and Sunday Morning*,
directed by Karel Reisz

CONTEMPORARY CINEMA

102 *L'Avventura*, directed by M. Antonioni

104 *Last Year in Marienbad*, directed by
Alain Resnais

106 *Bicycle Thieves*, directed by Vittorio
de Sica

108 Le Corbusier's *unité d'habitation* at Marseilles

ARCHITECTURE

The difficulty of creating buildings of a new type presented town-planners, architects and engineers with problems which were probably insoluble. It was necessary to reconcile the modern taste with the demands of quick and cheap reconstruction. Thus there were two very different building categories: on the one hand, those where the artist was not hampered in expressing himself, and on the other, vast constructions in the 'international style', identical in all continents and climates no matter how absurd this uniformity might be in certain countries. Expedients hastily conceived to house the crowds that streamed towards the cities, the latter are generally composed of large uniform blocks, and have the same regular, monotonous and somehow depersonalized structure. The only differences are those due to the variety of local materials used, but it is impossible at first glance to see the national characteristics of each country. Industrial civilization demands the standardization of collective buildings, as much in the materials used in their construction as in their plans. Uniform office-blocks and uniform housing are prefabricated or manufactured in standard units, and the materials that go into them are steel girders and beams, reinforced concrete, glass, plastics, cinder-blocks. There is a choice between a bearing framework with light cladding, or a self-bearing exterior, a combination of concrete and

110 Below, the Pirelli head office, Milan

111 Right, the Phoenix-Rheinrohr headquarters building, Düsseldorf

109 The Termini railway station at Rome

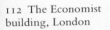

112 The Economist building, London

steel, with vinyl-resin roofing on an aluminium network. Standardization has been the rule, and façades are generally drab and glum.

Examples of a really new style are found only in the few countries with a high standard of living, and where, with little or no limitation of space, cities can expand in a rational manner. This is the case in Scandinavia, where the types of houses are adapted to their surroundings, and in Finland, where bricks and unpainted wood are harmoniously combined. In the same way Switzerland has been able to produce in Halen, near Berne, terrace houses with well-shaped balconies affording a view of the whole valley. France has had some of the worst architects in the post-war period, but also the greatest of all; yet it was only after his death that Le Corbusier was properly appreciated. In his *Unité d'habitation* at Marseilles, he popularized the principles of modern architecture by realizing his concept of the vertical street, the roof becoming the public place and the façades facing the sea on one side and the parched mountain on the other. His influence has been great, particularly on Eugène Beaudouin and Marcel Lods, who constructed at Rouen a complex of five hundred apartments with complete separation of motor traffic, pedestrians, schools and shopping-centre. Aillaud, at Bobigny and Aubervilliers,

113 St Catherine's College, Oxford

114 Sussex University

experimented with circular apartment towers and six-storey façades on a curved plan.

Buildings for collective use, such as schools, churches, factories and laboratories, have profited most from the work of new architects. Several examples are worth particular mention. In Great Britain, which remained exceedingly traditionalist for a long time, there is the new St Catherine's College at Oxford, as well as such handsome successes as Castrol House, the Economist building by Alison and Peter Smithson (1961), the Universities of Sussex and York. In West Germany there are the triple construction of the Thyssen offices in Düsseldorf, one of the most beautiful skyscrapers in Europe; several churches in the south; the Philharmonic Concert Hall in Berlin by Hans Scharoun, which has been called a triumph of the principles of functional architecture, everything in its design being subordinated to the aim of providing perfect acoustics; the Maria Königin church in Saarbrücken. In the Netherlands there are the already-mentioned Lijnbann in Rotterdam and the children's centre by Aldo van Eyck near Amsterdam; in Italy, the sports arena and the Termini Station of Rome, and in Milan the Pirelli building; in France, the UNESCO building in Paris, Le Corbusier's church at Ronchamp and his chapel for the La Tourette monastery near Lyons, the church of Sainte Agnès at Fontaine-les-Grès, the University of Caen, the Medical School at Marseilles. There are also a number of factories and office-buildings where an attempt has been made to reduce austerity by mixing green areas with the buildings: the Olivetti factories at Ivrea, the Fors factories in Sweden, those of Ballerup in Denmark, the electricity centre of La Bathie, the Sandoz laboratories in Orléans.

The USSR has remained faithful to neo-classical academic architecture, with its colonnades, its classical pediments and Corinthian columns, of which Moscow University is the most typical example. It would seem that this type of architecture will have to be renounced in favour of the concepts that have won out in other countries.

RELIGIOUS LIFE

Religious activity and belief has been deeply affected, whether in the liberal democratic countries or the People's Democracies. It would have been unthinkable for the powerful churches to continue to ignore the considerable changes wrought in people's mentality and their modes of life by industrial civilization and its consequences.

It is worth noting that if, on the whole, the religious influence of the churches has greatly diminished – though, in a parallel way, anticlericalism also is on the wane – there have remained and indeed expanded, outside of the great religions, a kind of diffuse religiosity and a trend towards belief in the supernatural, as well as an authentic mysticism which results from the retreat from rationalism. The proliferation and extension of sects attests to the search for new paths of salvation and mystical satisfaction, which the traditional religions are no longer equipped to provide. Leaving aside charlatans, who exploit the credulity of simple people – pseudo-fakirs, clairvoyants, astrologists – we may point to the Buddhist and Hindu-inspired sects which have their missionaries in Europe, the spread of the Christian Science Church, the 'Christ of Montfavet' movement, Jehovah's Witnesses and Seventh-Day Adventists, whose adherents are generally modest people, undemanding from the intellectual point of view but eager to find a human community that corresponds to their spiritual needs. This is true also of the frequent conversions from one Christian Church to another, and even to Judaism. An analogous phenomenon is the emergence and branching out of numerous small Protestant groups in southern Italy and Sicily.

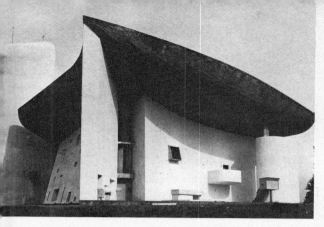

115 Left above, church at Ronchamp by Le Corbusier

116 Above, Notre Dame de Royan

117 Left, Nouvelle Eglise Saint Pie X, Lourdes

118 Left below, Coventry Cathedral

119 Below, Maria Königin church, Saarbrücken

In spite of its overall unity, the Catholic Church in Europe shows very clear national variations. It is impossible to draw a map showing the distribution of religions effectively practised in Europe; for one thing, we are unable to distinguish the true fervour and authentic practice of a religion from the simple, automatic observance of rites and customs. Besides, many countries do not take a census of religious affiliation, and many who declare officially that they belong to a religion practise it either desultorily or not at all. Most common is 'seasonal conformity', i.e. the observance of religious uses at moments in life that are considered important: baptism, first communion, marriage, funerals. In countries like France, Italy and Spain, which official statistics represent as fundamentally Catholic, there are large non-practising sectors: in Rome, only 10 per cent of men observe Easter communion, in Madrid 5 per cent, in Paris only 5 to 15 per cent (according to district) go to Mass. The considerable importance of non-practising Catholics (even though they may declare themselves, often for conformity's sake, as believers) is clear from a growing number of works of religious sociology. And the same observation applies to the various Protestant churches, since it is estimated that only 5 per cent of the English, and 20 per cent of the Scottish population, are more or less effectively practising churchgoers.

Another significant index is the drop in religious vocations and the increasing age of the clergy, including monks and nuns. For example, in the diocese of Metz, one of the most devout in France, only 8 per cent of monks are less than 30 years old, and the average age is 55. In the whole of France, between 1953 and 1956, the number of ordinations reached 4,150, while 5,032 priests died; and during 1968 some 145 priests abandoned their orders. In Spain, the number of novices entering seminaries in 1968 was over 1,000 fewer than in 1961. In 1967, 80 Franciscans in Verona left their monastery. A number of dioceses have had to regroup in order to combine their seminaries into one, and this has affected convents, too.

The decline of religious observance is more marked in cities, where social pressure to conform is not so great as in the country. But there is evidence that the 'crisis of faith' is general. Perhaps this is compensated for by a deeper and more authentic religious sense among those who continue to practise their religion, purged of many medieval customs and rites. Uneducated people, however, adhere to such traditions, because they see in them the essence of religion. Hence the situation is paradoxical. On the one hand, the Catholic

Church, in the person of its head, the pope, and the bishops, is generally the object of respect, consideration and indeed favours which many governments at the end of the nineteenth century would have refused it; on the other hand, governments and the ruling classes pay little attention to the precepts of the Gospel. Nor do they heed the pope's denunciations of atomic weapons and appeals for disarmament, any more than they do the bishops' exhortations to respect social justice and carry out a reform of the social structure.

In the face of such a decline in religion, the most far-seeing leaders of the Church have considered it imperative to keep step with the changes brought about by industrial civilization, the world-wide increase in urbanization and the growing influence of the working class. We must add to this the fear of Communism, declared by Pius XII to be 'intrinsically wicked'. During his pontificate the Church remained an absolute monarchy, made more rigidly authoritarian by the influence of reactionary Cardinals who were obstinately hostile to change. The election of John XXIII inaugurated a shift which many thought would be complete; the new pope called a Council, which, after an adjournment, met in 1962.

For a long time, far-sighted Catholics had understood that it was impossible to maintain the principles affirmed by the *Syllabus*, which declared war on all modern liberties. They asked for much greater freedom in theological and liturgical matters, especially in countries where the Catholic masses were the most enlightened: Germany, France, the Netherlands and Great Britain. Similarly, the visible divorce between the Church and the mass of the people demanded the use of methods of disseminating the faith that were better suited to the conditions of modern life. Finally, the preservation of clerical authority over the faithful, kept under guardianship and allowed no participation in decisions which directly affected them, explained in large measure the discredit of the Church in certain European countries and the necessity for new initiatives, such as the 'French Mission' (1941) and the 'Paris Mission' (1944). Thus there was a general thrust of the Church towards the world. But this disturbed Pius XII and led him to multiply his condemnations of Communism and his interdictions against any new forms of the apostolate (e.g. the worker-priests). At the same time the encyclical *Humani generis* (1950) denounced the dangers of historicity, and the pontifical Academy of Theology criticized the philosophy of the Jesuit father Teilhard de Chardin, forbidding him to write for several years.

At the Council, a reformist majority emerged, led by the German, Dutch, French, Belgian and English cardinals, and various South American and African bishops. They brought valuable support to reformist circles; apart from strictly religious decisions, they adopted an attitude that was clearly favourable to greater openness towards the world, and to the abandonment of everything which might hinder a dialogue 'and understanding between the Church and non-Catholics, even complete non-believers. Thus the encyclical *Pacem in terris* explicitly supported the United Nations Declaration of Human Rights and declared that cooperation was possible 'in economic, social and political spheres', even with those who instil 'false doctrines' (which remain condemned); this was supplemented by Paul VI's encyclical *Mater et magistra*, which declared a policy of socialization permissible; religious liberty was formally proclaimed, and the Holy Office and the Index were suppressed.

Since 1964 the reactionaries have sought to mount a counter-offensive. Nevertheless, a profound reform movement has been launched, and controversy has been introduced into the Church. The lower clergy, in particular, refuse to shelve the Council's decisions on free expression of thought and make full use of them at the diocesan synods which enable them to participate in administration with the bishop, who used to be sovereign master. There have been demonstrations, unthinkable in the past, which have gone as far as the occupation of churches (at Parma, in Spain, in the Netherlands), unauthorized meetings of hundreds of protesting priests, petitions against celibacy of the priesthood and in favour of contraception, etc. In short, the crisis of authority, spreading all over the world and in all spheres, has even affected the social body that has traditionally been the most hierarchical and was, for centuries, the rock on which all schisms were crushed.

The Protestant churches are not immune to this same movement, but their less rigid structure and the variety of their forms make the breaches less evident. Here, too, the number of the faithful who practise in the spirit as well as in the letter, has decreased, varying according to sect. In Sweden, where 86 per cent of babies are still baptized, the recruitment of clergymen is difficult and certain churches have had to resign themselves to the ordination of female pastors. The number of divorces increases, and contraception, accepted in any case by various churches (notably the Anglican Church in Britain), is widely used. A conservative tendency also exists in the Protestant churches of which Karl Barth, one of the most influential Christian thinkers, is the most eminent representative. It was he who put the Catholics on guard against the example of nineteenth-century liberal Protestantism, which preferred a 'dialogue with the world' to the proclamation of the Gospel, who pointed to the dangers of 'renewing the church through the light of modernity and not through the light of the Gospel'.

In Great Britain the many non-conformist churches form an active federation, so that the official Church is 'no longer more than a minority within a minority'. In Germany the Protestant Church divided in two during the war: one was the confessing Church, with pastor Niemöller and Karl Barth (until he went into exile at Basle), which was hostile to Nazism and became clandestine; the other the German Christians, who rallied to the Nazi cause. They reunited after the defeat into one Evangelical Church; alongside them remain the free territorial Lutheran churches, which are again separated because there are two Germanies.

The Second Vatican Council made an effort to bring the Catholic and the other Christian churches closer together. Until then, Catholics had rigorously maintained positions strongly disputed by Protestants. As the result of concessions on important points – veneration of the Virgin Mary, mixed marriages, adoption of the vernacular in place of Latin, recognition for the first time of some papal responsibility for the eastern schism, and abandonment of a number of polemical assaults on the Protestant Reformation – friendly relations were established not only with the Protestants, but also with the Greek Orthodox Church (as shown by Paul VI's visit to the Patriarch of Constantinople, Athenagoras) and even with the Russian Church. Nevertheless, the Roman Catholic Church remains on the whole hostile to divorce and birth-control (witness the encyclical *Populorum progressio*).

This more liberal attitude is one of the reasons for the *détente* which is developing between the Vatican and the Communist states. A *modus vivendi* has been established with some of them: countries in which the Catholics are either a majority (Poland), a strong minority (Yugoslavia, Czechoslovakia), or indeed small in number (Rumania). Negotiations have also begun recently with Hungary. In Poland, where the Church wields great power over the peasant masses, it defends its privileges and independence with great persistence and success and virtually constitutes a state within the state.

In the USSR, active pro-atheist propaganda, which was soft-pedalled during the war, oscillates between revivals of activity and calmer periods. In any case, the great majority of the population, who were born since 1917 and never received a religious education except in the bosom of families retaining their faith, are detached from religious observance. In 1957 there were reported to be 2,000 churches, 35,000 priests, 8,000 monks in all and 30,000,000 practising Orthodox churchgoers. But the evidence is contradictory: some reports indicate that the churches are filled with the faithful (which may well be true since few are open for worship), others that services are attended by only a scattering of people, most of them old. Lutheran and Calvinist churches have long disappeared, and the only sects that remain are the Mennonites (20,000), many of whom retreated with the Germans in 1943, the Baptists (520,000) and the Seventh-Day Adventists (25,000).

The Jews, mercilessly decimated during the Nazi occupation, have made some recovery, particularly in France, where most of those who left North Africa, and chose not to go to Israel, have been installed. The six-days' war in 1967 has had complicated and contradictory repercussions in the countries of eastern Europe, one of which has been a certain revival of anti-Semitism, accompanied by occasional outrages against Jewish property.

120 The reactionary Church: Danish cartoon (1967)

V THE WEAKNESSES

The Europe we have described – a Europe which has experienced a rapid renaissance of unexpected dimensions, a self-evident rise in general standards of living, an unquestionable growth of prosperity, greater than any before, in any period of human history – this Europe, whose social peace is relatively more secure than at many moments in the past, nevertheless shows signs of uneasiness and insecurity. Its prosperity, the approximation towards what Saint Just called the 'right to happiness', are fragile and at the mercy of minor incidents. The crisis of 1968 demonstrated the precariousness of economic stability and the superficiality of social appeasement; nor can one ignore armed conflicts, the open or civil warfare (in the form of guerrilla activity) which desolate certain continents and in which the great European powers are not entirely disinterested.

The economy
The weaknesses are apparent in various spheres, but first of all in the economy. It is true that the world has not re-experienced a catastrophic depression like the one which, in most countries of Europe, particularly in France, continued from 1930 up to the eve of the Second World War, and which some economists believe was only dispelled by re-armament and later by the immense needs of reconstruction. But the European economy in the post-war period has gone through periodic recessions of a peculiar kind. They are not caused, as was believed before the war, by overproduction, but by unplanned production and, even more important, by under-consumption. These recessions raise fears of the recurrence of a general economic crisis on the scale of the pre-war depression, whose ghost is not yet laid. They are also a reminder that the great threat hanging over the European economy is inflation, which governments seek to avert by a policy first of expansion and then austerity. This is the 'stop-go' system in current use. We must also note the economic weaknesses from

167

which certain countries suffer – particularly Great Britain, whose chronic crises affect the daily life of industry and business, and naturally that of all citizens; and also France, whose slow expansion and difficulties in modernization (the excessive number of unprofitable rural small holdings, the preponderance of small shopkeepers and businesses that weigh down the flow of trade and keep prices high) are plain to see. The sterling area is frequently threatened by the decline in the price of raw materials, and the fall of the pound is checked only for short periods, usually by raising the discount rate or by devaluation. Recently even countries whose economic expansion seemed irresistible – Italy, West Germany, the United States – have suddenly been threatened with monetary crises which forced their leaders to exercise great vigilance and sometimes to take drastic measures in order to head them off.

International uneasiness

There is also the burden – and perhaps this is the main cause of the economic difficulties – imposed by international insecurity, which forces all countries to maintain and increase heavy military expenditures. Even though the wars of colonial reconquest are over (except for Portugal, engaged in a hopeless delaying action in Angola and Mozambique), military expenditure remains at an almost insupportable level, both for traditional armies and for nuclear armaments, although the latter are pointless for the European powers, in view of the lead which the two super-powers have already achieved and their immense superiority in resources and industrial capacity. In the Hellenistic era, the appearance of great mercenary armies made a mockery of the rivalries between the Greek city-states and led to their degeneration into dependencies of the powerful oriental monarchies or of Rome. Today there is a similar threat to the independence of the great European powers – Great Britain, Germany and France – and to their former preponderance in world affairs. Instead the preponderant role is passing to the two super-powers, the USA and the USSR, which will eventually, no doubt, be joined by China – that is to say, those powers which can support the burden of research and armament expenditure, and are capable of vying in the sphere of nuclear arms and space-programmes. For most 'small' countries who attempt to compete, the diversion of enormous sums to military ends and prestige has no practical use and does harm to their economic growth, their social resources and the level of national consumption.

Demography

Another of Europe's weaknesses – and not the least disturbing – is the relative slowness of its demographic growth, which adversely influences its economic progress. The resulting demographic imbalance is pronounced in spite of an increase in the European population which appeared very promising immediately after the war, but recently has become very sluggish. Mortality in western Europe, particularly infant mortality, was lower in 1950 than in the years 1930–38, and the curve has continued to descend since then. We have seen that the birth-rate in the immediate post-war period was higher than before 1939, except in West Germany, Italy and Belgium, but since 1963 it has clearly been declining, and this is a general phenomenon, involving not only countries which were in the war but also those which remained neutral.

At first this growth was welcomed, but later many people, including certain governments, feared that the population surplus might create considerable future problems. In fact, the increase in the number of old people and of those under 18 (who are not yet of working age) places burdens on the working population – the only truly productive element – that threaten to become intolerable. This is the reason for the extension of family-planning projects and the abolition of laws prohibiting dissemination of information about contraception, thus freeing women from unbearable conditions which could even endanger their lives. However, in countries where Catholic influence is strong, which are often those where the standard of living is lowest, family-planning still runs up against strict prohibitions and deeply rooted social prejudices. This is a vital problem to which all countries must be forced to adopt the obvious, rational solution.

The eastern countries experienced the same growth, all the more marked since it affected populations which (except in East Germany) were still in large part rural. In the USSR, however, the birth-rate has dropped, particularly since 1960, and the percentage of men of 60 years and more has risen from 6.8 to 9.4. In the People's Democracies, which have become less predominantly rural because of increased industrialization, urbanization has made rapid progress, with the result that both the birth-rate and the mortality-rate have dropped significantly. Although there are still great differences between one country and another, the rate of increase has fallen sharply everywhere in the east, except for Poland.

169

This situation becomes more meaningful if one compares it with that in various other countries in the world. For instance, the mortality-rate in the United States dropped between 1940–50 and 1964, but there was an astounding 'baby-boom' right after the Second World War. It is true that the birth-rate has consistently declined since 1957, as the use of contraception became more common – so that the age structure resembles that of western Europe. But the situation is more favourable there than it was in Europe during the 1930–40 period because of the increasing youthfulness of the population, in spite of the fact that the proportion of older people continues to grow. But the more significant contrasts with Europe occur elsewhere. In Canada, where the French-speaking population is the most prolific, the natural rate of growth is considerable (1·5 per cent in 1964) and immigration also plays a part; in Australia the growth-rate has been 2·2 per cent, mostly due to immigration. In Israel, the legislation granting Jews free entry to their 'national home' resulted in sizable immigration and the growth-rate reached 3·7 per cent between 1961 and 1966, with a very large proportion of youngsters and people between the ages of 15 and 49. In Asia, Japan is the only exception, because of the very strong birth-control movement there; neverthe-less, in 1967 it still had 100,000,000 inhabitants, with a density of 165 per sq. km. As rural overpopulation is always pressing in Japan, the result is the arrival in the cities of around a million additional workers a year.

In the underdeveloped countries, the contrast is marked. There is no population decline here but rather a substantial increase of births accompanied by a sharp drop in mortality. Whereas the rate of growth has remained well below 0·9 per cent in Europe, it reached 2·4 per cent in Africa as a whole between 1960 and 1962, 2·9 and 2·7 per cent in Central and South America, 2·7 in South East Asia. In Indonesia the rate of growth is 2·2 per cent (Java increased its population by 15,000,000 between 1940 and 1957), and 30 to 40 per cent of the working population is unemployed or underemployed. Malaysia had a growth-rate of 3·2 per cent from 1958 to 1962, Ceylon 3·1 per cent from 1953 to 1956 and 2·7 per cent from 1958 to 1962. In India and Pakistan the situation is almost catastrophic with a growth-rate of 2·5 per cent.

The demographic rise in China is also remarkable. At least 40 per cent of the population is under 17 years of age. The rate of growth is still 2 per cent, in spite of a birth-control campaign that began in

1956 with contraception and even legal abortion. Though the birth-rate has declined, the mortality-rate, especially of infants, also dropped to 110 in 1957 despite war, revolutions, famines and increasing urbanization.

Throughout the underdeveloped world, the young are particularly numerous: in Nigeria 40 per cent are under 14 years old, among the Kikuyu in Kenya 42 per cent. In Algeria 53 per cent of the population are under 19, and only 5 per cent are over 60. This is true also in Madagascar, where those under 19 comprise 42·5 per cent of the population while those over 65 are 3·2 per cent (compared with 12·5 per cent in France).

In sum, whereas the population of Europe increased by only 35,000,000 between 1945 and 1960, that of Latin America grew by 56,000,000, that of Africa by 61,000,000, and that of Asia by 337,000,000. These figures demonstrate how far the weight of Europe has diminished in an awakening world where the production potential is considerable, even if the population density of some countries remains small.

Financial problems
A more immediate danger is posed by the latent monetary crisis, which is revealed in a spectacular way by the difficulties that have agitated several western European stock-exchanges for some years.

121, 122 German and Polish posters advocating birth control

123 German cartoon on the relationship between the franc and the Deutsche Mark (1957)

125 Opposite page, the deserted London Stock Exchange, 15 March 1968

126 Opposite below, re-opening of Paris Bourse after seven-day closure in November 1968

"YOU KNOW, I'M BEGINNING TO FEEL THIS NATIONAL
SPORT'S GETTING REALLY CRUEL . . ."

28th Mar., 1963:   The Grand National again

124 British cartoon on the recurring financial crisis

This is the great dispute about the gold standard, the monetary system which puts certain currencies on a parity with gold, and has been the basis of world economy for almost fifty years. As everyone knows, apart from a certain reserve of gold, the central banks hold large supplies of hard currency to guarantee the paper money which, in practice, is all that is put into circulation: for this purpose the dollar and the Swiss franc are considered to have retained their value in gold. But since each of the various countries, including the United States,

1964

1965

1966

1967

1967

1968

1968

127 'There was an old woman who swallowed a fly . . .': cartoon showing
Britain's increasingly difficult economic position ▶

has its own autonomous monetary policy, and since some economists believe that the system inevitably involves a concealed inflation, there is a tendency for the flight of capital to the hard-currency countries. This influx of speculative capital became so serious in West Germany in 1968–69 that the government had to revalue the Deutsche Mark, re-establish export subsidies, and place restrictions on agricultural imports. On the other hand, certain countries, under the pressure of inflation, have had to increase their issue of paper money. Both Great Britain and France have twice been forced to undertake devaluations which so unsettled their economy that the stock-exchange had to be closed for several days. Countries that hold considerable reserves of specie almost inevitably exert pressure on the currencies of their satellites when they devalue, and this causes serious disturbances to the monetary systems of these dependent states. Examples of this were seen when the pound was devalued in December 1967 and the French franc in 1969. This absence of monetary stability and the lack of coordination between different national economic policies is one factor hindering the establishment of a true common market. Moreover, the West German revaluation confirmed the supremacy of the dollar as the sole standard. In 1969, more than ever, the dollar had become the hard currency *par excellence* and enjoys a primacy comparable to that immediately after the war.

The absence of fiscal unity in Europe is another serious weakness. The tax system of each country bears little relation to those of its neighbours. For example, the burden of indirect taxes is heavier in France than elsewhere and tax evasion reigns supreme there; estimated in terms of dollars, indirect taxes in France are equivalent to 468, in West Germany 450, in Belgium 373, in the Netherlands 358, and in Italy 219. Unification presupposes thorough reform of very old traditions which would offend many vested interests; nevertheless, it is indispensable if a European union is to be achieved.

Nationalism
Divided on the ideological plane into two worlds with different economic foundations and correspondingly different social structures, Europe is also – and more seriously – divided by another threat. Nationalism, far from weakening after the lessons of the Second World War, shows signs of regaining and even increasing its strength. In spite of its dominant role in the origins of two world wars, it has not yet been appeased. This is shown by the emergence of various

Fascist parties: the neo-Fascists in Italy (the Italian Social Party), the NPD in West Germany, clandestine organizations in other countries, as well as the nationalist government in Lisbon which seeks to maintain rebellious colonies under Portuguese authority in liaison with the racist states of Rhodesia and the Union of South Africa. In addition, there is Franco's nationalism which exploits the Gibraltar problem in order to divert attention from internal difficulties in Spain, and the far from negligible resurgence of anti-Semitism which is nourished in certain circles by the policies of Israel.

In many countries the teaching of history is still governed by preoccupations foreign to pure knowledge of the past. Too often mixed with civic instruction, history is becoming a school for the formation of a patriotism exalting ancient glories and passing in silence over the dark pages which have marked the pasts of all countries at one time or another. Every state more or less openly professes the formula, 'My country, right or wrong': thus children's minds are deformed by ignorance or misunderstanding of other countries and the idealization of their own. UNESCO has sponsored conferences of history teachers from countries that were formerly hostile, with the object of studying text-books in current use, particularly their points of difference and, most important, their distortions and falsifications. Agreement on such points has been easy among scholars of good faith, but their resolutions have no effective power. One must look to the better training of schoolmasters (and publishers) for the disappearance of this nationalism, which gives children wrong attitudes and causes contempt for or fear of the foreigner. These dangerous falsifications are often linked with the large-circulation press, always prompt to pander to the lowest instincts of uninformed people – particularly by putting the blame on foreigners for provoking conflicts and for the difficulties of their own government. In the hands of political, religious or social pressure groups – sometimes foreign ones – the press can be one of the most powerful instruments for fomenting discord, whereas its role ought to be the objective presentation of events, and a contribution towards better understanding among people.

The difficulties encountered in setting up defensive military organizations on both sides of the Iron Curtain – NATO on the one side and the Warsaw Pact organization on the other – have shown how precarious they are. In some circles of West Germany, one can detect hopes of revenge, the aim being not only reunification of the country but also recovery of the territory lost to Poland and the USSR. Although the old Franco-German hostility has died down, there is still a certain mistrust, manifested in France's refusal to allow Germany to be equipped with nuclear arms and in French fears of being drawn into a war of revenge.

Nationalism in France is more or less encouraged by the regime of the Fifth Republic; the most obvious example of this is the 'policy of grandeur'. This sentiment of the French head of state, anxious to remain master of his country's policies, was seen particularly in the French withdrawal from NATO and in unconcealed hostility towards the English-speaking world. While the Common Market has achieved considerable progress in the economic sphere to the great profit of its members, and agreements advantageous to all have been reached in particular fields, extremely bitter controversies have been far from infrequent, showing the strength of vested interests in those countries whose products are competitive (Italy and France in certain areas,

128, 129 Reviving nationalism. Above, Welsh separatist demonstration in Liverpool, 1965; right, students' rally at Nuremberg, 1961

130 Destruction in Budapest during the rising of 1956

131 Insurrection in East Berlin, 1953

France and Germany in others). General de Gaulle's brusque veto of Great Britain's application to join the Common Market (desirable for political reasons but bound to raise difficult economic problems) and the time-honoured tradition of protectionism in France cause some reservations when it comes to measures indispensable to the achievement of complete and effective agreement. And yet it is in the economic field that the most important successes have been realized. In the political sphere the French government is utterly opposed to the creation of any kind of super-state which would limit the autonomy of its members.

The fact that almost identical political and social regimes have been established in all the eastern European countries under Soviet influence has not prevented the rise of nationalism there, too. This is due, on the one hand, to a desire to escape from the exclusive domination of the USSR, and on the other, to the existence of historical traditions which partially explain the resistance and even the revolts which have occurred in East Germany, Hungary and Czechoslovakia – without forgetting the breakaway of Yugoslavia and, more recently, of Albania. Rumania's refusal to take part in the 1969 meeting of Warsaw Pact heads of state, and its forthright disapproval of the military occupation of Czechoslovakia, illustrate that country's desire for greater independence and the existence of a vigorous nationalism.

But within all European countries there are forces of local particularism and nationalism, which made themselves felt in the former Danish possession of Iceland (1944) and even in the Faroe Islands (1960). There are similar manifestations in Scotland, Wales and Northern Ireland and in Brittany, though these cannot as yet be compared with the strong national feeling of the Basque and Catalan peoples in Spain. National conflicts on a smaller scale have led to the independence of Malta (1964) and the establishment within the Italian Republic of autonomous provincial administrations for the Val d'Aosta, Sardinia and Sicily; but if these could be settled by negotiation, the Austrians of the South Tyrol have had recourse to terrorism in their struggle against the Italianization of that territory. The Hungarian and German minorities inside Rumania do not conceal their desire for greater autonomy – at least cultural – than they enjoy at present. In the Federal Republic of Yugoslavia, the Albanians in the autonomous province of Kosmet and certain Macedonians (whose country is divided among Yugoslavia, Bulgaria and Greece, but the majority of whom form one of the federated

Yugoslav republics) wish to be reunited in an independent state of their own. Even the French-speaking people of the Swiss Jura reject any constitutional provisions made without their consent, and have launched peaceful demonstrations for autonomy against the federal government in Berne. Elsewhere, on the other hand, the struggle has become violent. In Northern Ireland, there is virtually a state of civil war between Protestants and Catholics, the latter wishing to restore the political unity of the island. In Belgium there is a fierce collision between the Flemings and the Walloons, the strong Flemish birth-rate accentuating the numerical inequality between these two peoples. While the linguistic problem is the symbol here, it is also religious (Catholicism being all-powerful in the Flemish area), political and economic (the Walloons being predominantly liberal and Socialist); it has divided the country from top to bottom ánd defies solution principally because of the intransigence of the Flemish majority.

These seeds of discontent have existed practically everywhere at all times, but the instances we have mentioned attest to the revival of a dangerous state of mind, capable of disturbing social and even international peace.

The retreat of the democratic ideal
The weakness of Europe has penetrated also to the moral sphere – the sphere to which it owed its prestige, and continues to owe whatever prestige it still retains. This prestige rests on the ideals propounded by the French *philosophes* of the eighteenth century: ideals of tolerance, of liberty and equality, and of the right of men to rule themselves. The French Revolution spread these ideals throughout Europe, and all the peoples of the world derived from them the principles and aspirations which guided them in obtaining their independence. It was from European writers and European history that the 'educated' classes of South America, Africa and Asia learned these principles; European missionaries and Marxist propagandists spread ideologies of European origin; even when its dominion ceased, it was still Europe which had inculcated the means of emancipation. In newly independent countries, governments retained the administrative institutions created by the colonial powers and adopted a system of parliamentary democracy on the British or French pattern. In the sequel, these borrowed structures were often quickly battered down by tribal rivalries, personal ambitions, the corruption of civil servants and statesmen; and today one-party control and military dictatorship

are the rule. The prestige of Europe has suffered correspondingly. Yet at present, Europe – along with the United States – provides subsidies, industrial technicians, and agricultural experts, and teachers at all levels, without which these countries would be unable to survive.

But the most serious thing is that Europe itself has begun to change and is evolving along the same path as its former dependencies. Everywhere one can see the decline of parliamentary democracy. There is the example of Salazar's brutal dictatorship in Portugal, which benefits from the great powers' complaisance and keeps the country so stagnant economically that its standard of living is the lowest in Europe. The dictatorship of Franco makes only a few, essentially formal and inadequate, concessions in favour of the Protestants and Jews in the hope of receiving foreign capital and being admitted into the EEC. The savage military dictatorship of the 'colonels' in Greece decimates the country's intellectual élite. There is also a trend towards the personalization of power which recalls Stalin's 'cult of personality', notably in France where the existence of a 'reserved domain' on military questions and foreign affairs, and an electoral system that carves up the country to further the interests of power, have created a virtual monarchy, elective, to be sure, but in which a misconceived referendum system and the docility of a National Assembly elected on the personal appeal of a single individual reduce democracy to a mere façade.

Through the adroit manipulation of voting districts, the electoral systems in many countries are so unequal that a majority of representatives is often chosen by a minority of voters. The trend towards the rigid discipline of majorities makes it impossible for minorities to obtain support for their views. These are among the new traits of European politics, so different from those of classical parliamentary democracy, which show a more or less explicit tendency towards dictatorship. This has already gone as far as the prohibition of certain political parties (e.g., the Communist Party in West Germany from 1956 to 1969), thus depriving a fraction of the population of its right to be represented. There is also the growing influence of the United States, which openly favours the conservative parties in Germany, Italy and France, as well as the dictatorships of Portugal, Spain and Greece. The split of Socialist parties into at least two factions (in which the American trade unions played a very important role), the multifarious activities of the CIA in press matters, and American influence on military chiefs through personal relations formed within

132 Soviet cartoon on military government in Greece (1968)

NATO – all these factors have helped to put less democratic, less liberal governments in office and have contributed to the ascendancy of the military.

The cult of violence and intolerance

The retreat of liberalism appears even more clearly in the growing power of the police and the contempt for individual rights, once the greatest achievement of European civilization. Thus there is a cult of violence, as in the massacres of prisoners and the atrocities committed during the colonial wars (Kenya, Indo-China, Algeria, Katanga and the Kinshasa region), but its traces are visible everywhere. It is not a matter of isolated acts of violence due to the irrational impulse of an individual out of control, but of violence systematically organized. A form of sanctioned terrorism is exercised through threats against persons or property with the aim of discouraging the adversary, through direct action which keeps a threat hanging over a suspect or

133 Anti-police poster, Paris, 1968

134 The police-state atmosphere

135 The influence of literature on the use of violence

his family, or through preventative arrest or 'protective custody', i.e. arbitrary detention, keeping the accused incommunicado, deprived of the help of any defender, and subjecting him not only to uninterrupted interrogation, night and day, which finally breaks his physical and moral resistance, but also often to highly sophisticated tortures. When there is open unrest, the police have recourse to such weapons as tear gas.

Novels, the new theatre and the cinema emphasize violence. Murder is common currency and the individual lives in the midst of a hallucinatory society. Spy-stories and thrillers are often the sole reading of millions of people; and an endless stream of gangster films, detective films and westerns detail the meticulous preparation of crimes and feature scenes in which revolvers and machine-guns figure large. There has been an extraordinary vogue for secret-agent adventures, of which James Bond is the prototype; and war films, after having extolled the Second World War, are concentrating on Vietnam. Shown in all countries, these films popularize the forms of banditry used by young delinquents, whose numbers grow alarmingly.

Is it surprising, in these conditions, that social conflicts – even though they have become much rarer – should quickly take on an extremely violent character, on the part of demonstrators as well as the forces of order? This has been particularly evident in peasant demonstrations and in the youth demonstrations which took place in 1968 in West Germany and Berlin, in Spain, France and Italy. Here it was the youngest age-groups who proved the most aggressive, no doubt because they are the most receptive to the influences of radio, television and cinema, familiarizing them with the adult world and with scenes of violence which have become everyday occurrences to them.

Misleading information
One of the great revolutions produced during these twenty-five years, with consequences which are often regrettable, is the extraordinary development of the mass media, especially radio and television. But one must also add the rise of a specialized press addressed to children and adolescents, and the use of provocative advertising. All of this constitutes a virtual 'counter-education', the antithesis of the traditional education received by children in schools, where most of the instruction is imparted methodically and at their own level, with the forethought and discretion necessary for an audience of

183

children. Television and radio, on the contrary, present ideas without preparation, in adult language, and without the least precaution to prevent the 'shock' that certain revelations or scenes may produce on children's minds or feelings.

The object of press and television is to strike the mind and imagination in a more lasting way than words; hence they are doubtless the most powerful instruments of distortion and 'conditioning' that exist today. For the most part, the mass media are misleading because they lack the independence that would enable them to be objective. Thus school education, which is still on the whole the only means of protecting children from conformity and fanaticism, is effectively counteracted by the mass media, and these are often in the hands of governments or (sometimes foreign) financial interests.

Radio and television are for the most part state services, subjected, like the cinema, to official censorship or to an auto-censorship imposed by journalists and film-makers themselves out of fear of legal proceedings or the refusal of authorization to show their films. The British Broadcasting Corporation seems to be the only example of a relatively free radio and television service, and even it has come under increasing criticism.

Thus the great pressure-groups defend their sometimes contradictory interests. Their intervention can be seen, for example, in the veto on the French film *La Religieuse* (based on Diderot) or in the interesting case of the Italian film *Teorema*, which received an award from the Italian Catholic Cinema Committee and was, at the same time, forbidden by the Italian government for being irreligious!

Theoretically the western press is completely free, but this freedom is fictitious, for in reality it is subjected to financial interests and sometimes to governmental pressures (pre-censorship, self-censorship, seizure of newspapers on various pretexts). In certain countries the press is itself responsible for the weakening of civic concern and public spirit, as well as for the cult of violence; in any case it seems indisputable that it no longer plays its proper role, which ought to be the objective informing of its readers. Having become a major industry that requires a great quantity of capital, the press has turned into a tributary of advertising. It is concentrated into giant businesses, whose principal preoccupation is financial success. As for the journals of opinion, they have become – with rare exceptions – commercial enterprises like any other, whose owners, if they are rich enough, can use them to express, within certain limits, a personal political line.

In France, the small and medium-sized newspapers, which still existed in the provinces before the Second World War, have been amalgamated or bought out; they are shared by the Hachette and Havas groups which allow them to retain a few distinguishing features in order to give the reader the illusion that he has freedom of choice and opinion.

The most spectacular battles for control of the press have taken place in Great Britain. In 1960 Lord Rothermere's group bought the *Star* and amalgamated it with the *Evening News*; at the same time the *News Chronicle* was fused with the *Daily Mail*, the group's morning paper. The struggle between the Canadian millionaire, Lord Thomson, and the Cecil King group (*Daily Mirror*) ended in favour of the latter, which also bought the *Daily Herald* and published it as the *Sun*; but in 1966 it was Lord Thomson who bought control of *The Times* and the *Sunday Times*, and the *Sun* has again changed hands. Of all the British press, only the *Guardian*, the *Observer*, the *Daily Telegraph* (which controls a number of provincial papers as well) and the *Financial Times* still seem to enjoy a certain independence.

In West Germany, concentration is less advanced, but the Axel Springer group controls nineteen newspapers in the Federal Republic and West Berlin, with a circulation of 18,000,000. The influence of this group has been violently contested (through attacks on its plants and the burning of its stocks in 1966) because of its arch-conservatism.

Italian newspapers, two-thirds of which are sold in the north, are concentrated geographically in a small number of cities. Each newspaper is generally the property of a single group, but circulations are small; only five papers reach over 200,000 readers.

To the influence of these dailies, generally conformist and pro-government, we must add that of the weeklies, the glossy magazines, and the sentimental press addressed to a feminine public. These are inspired by the same aims and their impact is considerable. Through vulgar and romantic nonsense, these organs, together with television, contribute on a major scale to turning the population into sheep.

The press in eastern Europe follows lines which have nothing in common with the west. The situation is the most straightforward in the USSR: it is a state press in the service of revolutionary ideology, and any counter-revolutionary act is punishable. Since 1953, however, it has begun to change and become more liberal. The daily of the Communist Party, *Pravda*, with a printing of 6,700,000, now publishes *feuilletons* and fairly accurate foreign news; it also reserves a considerable amount of space for letters to the editor and reports from factory correspondents, which draw attention to the inadequacies of the administration and the economy. There are also discussions among the various newspapers. In the same way – except currently for Czechoslovakia – a certain liberalization has become evident in the press of the People's Democracies.

The ideals, which had seemed to justify Europe's prestige and its mastery of the world, are thus in decline. Europe continues to enjoy a wide influence, but it is worth noting that the 'third world' no longer feels the same whole-hearted admiration for Europe as formerly, and seeks to rediscover its own traditions, which the whites destroyed. This is attested by the strength of animism and syncretic religions in central Africa; of Islam (which is not considered a foreign import), not only in the Near East but all the way to Indonesia and South Africa; and of Buddhism in Asia. Significantly, the progress of Islam in black Africa is far more rapid than that of the Christian churches. In the case of technology and science, it is usually the United States which has taken the place once occupied by Europe.

EXTERNAL WEAKNESSES

The weaknesses of Europe are not exclusively internal ones; they also find their origin in the new situation of Europe in a completely altered world. It is not only on the military and diplomatic planes that the nations of the world were, in the past, or are still, liable to confront one another. They have daily relations in the economic sphere, and it is there that their interdependence appears most clearly. The panic that seized all the stock-markets of the globe in 1968 at the threat of revaluation of the Deutsche Mark and devaluation of the French franc (and which was repeated when these two decisions were taken in 1969) demonstrated better than earlier examples that all economies are interdependent. Similarly, the difficulties of the pound and the French franc could not have been overcome, at several junctures, without the aid of the other principal countries, not out of philanthropy – no one is naive enough to believe that – but out of the concern of possessors of other currencies which would have been disturbed by too great a devaluation.

The economic predominance of the United States

We have seen that the spectacular recovery of western Europe was made possible by Marshall Aid – at least it would not have been so rapid otherwise – and by offshore military orders. But in the years following the re-establishment of the European economy, new problems appeared. Having become exporters again, the European economies needed protection against competition from the American colossus. While competing with one another, they also sought to keep to themselves their former colonial markets. American exporters, on the other hand, tried to overcome this competition by developing their predominance over the new, weak African states, and Japanese industry gained a high position (third, if not second) in the world economy. Though they occupy only 7 per cent of the habitable parts of the globe and comprise only 7 per cent of an estimated 3,000,000,000 world population, the 200,000,000 inhabitants of the USA have so large a share in production of almost all kinds that they can virtually fix prices and control the international market. The present average annual income per capita in the United States is $3,500, in western Europe $1,800, in the USSR $1,000; the gross earnings of American corporations have grown each year from 7·7 per cent in 1961 to 9·5 per cent in 1966. It is a rare country that can do without American financial assistance and avoid its conditions, political as well as military. A single example will show how exclusive this preponderance is. In March 1963, when the workers of the large United States copper refineries went on strike, it became necessary to import copper, principally for the production of armaments for the Vietnam war; as a result the price of copper doubled on the London market.

United States penetration of the underdeveloped world has often taken place in the guise of disinterested aid, but also in the form of overt military assistance. By a coincidence which can hardly be fortuitous, the principal, if not the only, beneficiaries of this aid are the former colonies whose geographic situation gives them considerable strategic or political importance (Burma, India, Pakistan, the Philippines, Uganda, Kenya, Congo-Kinshasa, Indonesia, Chad, and almost the whole of Latin America) or those which possess such valuable mineral reserves as uranium, oil, copper, tin, manganese, etc. It would be outside the scope of this book to discuss the multiple forms this aid takes and the means by which it is distributed. It should be remembered simply that the United States has an overwhelming capacity for expansion in most fields, and therefore competitive powers which it is almost impossible to withstand for long. The abundant capital of the giant corporations and banks of the United States, the superiority of its industrial and commercial technology, the methodical market research of its banks and analysis centres, the competence of its managers, the powerful assistance it derives on the spot from its military bases and diplomatic representatives who provide information, guide its investments, support it in every way and protect its interests in cases where unfavourable legislation is proposed – the result of all these types of action is a considerable imbalance between the United States and Europe.

Japan, in spite of the success of birth-control measures taken since 1955, is still an overpopulated country. After the reconstruction period it undertook intensive industrialization and its growth-rate has been the fastest in the world. It has become the third highest steel-producer, after the USA and the USSR, and the first in shipbuilding. In 1966 its rising chemical and heavy industries accounted for 59 per cent of total industrial activity. More than other countries it is forced to export at any price, but it is favoured in this by the low salaries of its work-force and by the abundance of capital which results from particularly high savings.

In Europe, where Japanese capital and manufactures (automobiles, textiles, transistors, etc.) are only just beginning to appear, it is still the United States alone which is able, through capital investment, to place the continent in a relatively colonial situation. As J. J. Servan-Schreiber has shown, it is by such means as more or less clandestine participation in European businesses, purchase of European patents which it exploits on the spot with much cheaper labour, direct pur-chases of firms, particularly those which, because of their advanced technology, have a strong growth coefficient, that American capital controls 15 per cent of consumer goods in Europe, 24 per cent of automobile manufacture, 20 per cent of light engineering and consu-mer durables (radios, televisions, cash-registers) and especially domi-nates the electronics field, where it controls 50 per cent of transmitter production, 80 per cent of computers, and 95 per cent of the market in integrated circuits, which make it possible to simplify computers and to make them stronger, smaller and lighter. This industry benefits from the considerable aid and credits that the American government devotes to research in the anticipation that electronics will play an almost exclusive role in the new future. Nor should we forget the 'brain-drain' to the United States of young people, mainly engineers

136, 137 Cartoons on American influence on western Europe: left, the rape of Europa; above, the American Army carrying weak Europe in its arms

138 The penetration of Japanese influence in Europe: an interior shown at the Brussels Expo of 1958

and technicians, whose compatriots have contributed at great expense to their scientific education, but who are attracted by higher salaries. At the same time, American businessmen have achieved a rational and balanced distribution of their plants (Belgium, the Netherlands, Spain). Between 1960 and 1965 American investment in industrial installations and equipment in Europe was one and a half times that which it invested in the rest of the world.

The results achieved by the EEC and the further developments anticipated have disturbed the United States, and led to its proposal of a general tariff revision. This is the so-called 'Kennedy Round', undertaken after a vote in 1962 authorizing the President to negotiate a lowering of American tariffs, which, as is well-known, are very high. This would open up Europe to American products with virtually no defence, and it would also deprive the EEC of its status as an independent 'third economic force' between the two super-powers. The negotiations, however, have reached an impasse, for the United States is unwilling to renounce its strict protectionism.

The dangers for Europe of depending on a foreign industry are manifold. Its plant will inevitably be less well maintained and replacements will have to be imported. The policy-making bodies located across the Atlantic will be able to decide, without the national governments' being capable of preventing it, to close or run down this or that factory, with the risk of provoking grave social crises. The export of profits offers a permanent means of pressure on exchange rates. Finally, American firms installed in Europe can create price wars, since their technological superiority allows them to achieve lower cost prices while often paying higher wages than those of their European competitors, and this brings on a general rise in wages. American capital is invested in highly industrialized countries, already well-equipped with superstructures and a qualified labour force (West Germany, France, Great Britain, the Netherlands), whose largest firms are nevertheless weak financially and show diminishing profit-margins. But it is invested also in those countries where industry is still relatively undeveloped, where labour is cheaper and the governments more docile (Spain, southern Italy, Ireland, Greece). These investments are either direct, or indirect through the intermediacy of German, Swiss or Italian firms.

Latin America, which was for long a preserve of British capital, has since 1923 become an increasingly guarded hunting-ground for United States capital and United States policy, which makes and unmakes governments at will. In Asia, Japanese exports (for which the United States is the primary supplier and customer) are directed towards neighbours in the Far East and the South-East; but they are already penetrating black Africa and the Near East, as well as South America and even China. This comprises an extremely large and highly populated zone, which is a predetermined client for products whose low prices make them preferable to European products. The result is that Japan's economic expansion limits and will increasingly limit the share that Europe has managed to preserve. Besides, Europe continues to recede politically and militarily: having lost its colonies, it is now abandoning its overseas bases – witness the British government's announcement of its progressive withdrawal from bases in the Indian Ocean before 1972.

The retreat in former overseas colonies
It is not only at home that the European countries are threatened by the penetration of American capital; this is true also in their former colonies, where they believed they could preserve control of the markets over which they had lost political dominion. At the moment, however, Europe is less badly placed in relation to the (mainly African) 'third world' than in relation to the United States. Even when it is itself threatened by virtual colonization, it is making every effort to maintain, under a disguised form, its former colonizing activities.

After obtaining independence, the new African and Asian states seemed to model themselves on their former colonizers. Thus the colonial powers nourished the illusion that, even while abandoning political positions that had become untenable and giving up the attributes of sovereignty, they could preserve the essential factor, that is, the profitable exploitation of natural resources and labour to feed their industry, as well as the old markets. Hence the insidious campaign to persuade the liberated populations that nationalism was an outdated concept and that it was in their interests to be associated in a large group. This was the thinking behind the drive for a Euro-Africa which would reserve for Europe the supply of industrial products and for the African states the supply of raw materials. It was nothing but an attempt to restore the colonial pact. In fact the new states have maintained (but for how long?) their economic, and particularly their financial, links with the former mother-country (in the sterling area and the French franc zone), as well as commercial

139 The last stages of resistance to African decolonization

relations; at the same time they seek to shake off excessive dependence by diversifying their suppliers and customers. They have therefore signed bilateral treaties with other countries for the trade of their commodities on better terms against products that are essential and cheaper. Military intervention in Vietnam and in North Africa, the Suez campaign and the war in the Belgian Congo have shown that the colonial powers were not disposed to renounce their privileged exploitation of former colonies without a struggle.

Political independence inevitably awakens a desire for economic independence, and that is what the new states are seeking. But Europe holds on to its vantage points, and is helped in this by the corruption of the new leaders, their misappropriation of funds, their expenditures on prestige and personal luxury. The extreme instability of governments in the 'third world', and the prevalence of civilian or military *coups d'état* and dictatorships cause constant intervention – openly or under cover – from outside. The present situation of Africa is like that of Spanish America in 1828: complete disorder leading to the reduction of essential food cultivation, and racial conflicts fostering emigration to Europe: from Kenya and Rhodesia to Great Britain, from Senegal and particularly North Africa to France. One of the results is to create great bitterness among those natives who return from Europe, where they have been able to measure the extent of the gulf that separates the two worlds.

In 1960 the Organization for European Economic Cooperation (OEEC), which had been set up in 1948, was transformed into the Organization of Economic Cooperation and Development (OECD), and established a Committee for Development Aid (CDA), in which West Germany joined. This aid takes various forms, such as financial loans (reaching the sum of $11,300,000,000 in 1967), postponement or remission of the repayment of old debts and outstanding debits on imports, subsidies for public expenditures (which imply a more or less effective measure of control), and technological assistance. Private investment is also an aspect of this scheme, but the insecurity and instability of the new governments make it hesitant. Credits are distributed for the Common Market countries by the European Development Fund (EDF) through the European Investment Bank (EIB). The European Development Fund replaced the French European Fund for Overseas Development (FEDOM) in 1963, after signature of the agreement which granted eighteen African and Malagasy states association in the Common Market. But the coordination of aid is still very poor, and the best results are obtained by the World Bank. In addition, aid is supplied by Sweden and Switzerland; by the USSR and the People's Democracies, which generally sign barter agreements or grant long delays of payment in kind at fixed prices over an extended period (sometimes five years); and also by Israel, Yugoslavia and China.

Virtually the entire African continent is in need of aid and guidance. Even in most of the newly independent North African countries, in spite of the bloody Algerian war, the European powers have retained positions that still appear to be solid, through maintenance of the sterling area and French franc zone. Great Britain reserves 85 per cent of its financial aid for Commonwealth countries; France 95 per cent for French franc zone countries; Belgium 98 per cent for Congo-Kinshasa, Ruandi and Burundi; Italy 50 per cent for Somaliland. As to technical aid, France sends mainly doctors, engineers and teachers. But the financial difficulties of France and Great Britain have forced them to cut back their financial aid. This aid often goes along with a military alliance, which provides not only training staffs for the local armies, but also troops on the spot, ready to intervene and lend their support to the local governments. In 1961, for instance, French troops supported President M'Ba of Gabon when he was threatened by revolution, and a little later they supported the government of Chad, just as British troops intervened in 1961 in Kenya and Tanganyika. The United States already has a solid West African base in Liberia, which is virtually an American colony; it intervened actively in the Congo affair, and its forces are present everywhere.

Slowly, however, industries are being created, and agriculture and the exploitation of raw materials are beginning to diversify and expand, lessening dependence on one commodity. But then over-production leads to a collapse of the market, while the large mining groups push their exploitation of mineral deposits to the point of exhaustion, leaving little profit to the mass population. The results are underemployment or unemployment, poverty, malnutrition and sickness which are evident in nearly sixty states where the gross national product per capita is less than $250 a year. In addition, the European and North American powers have consistently refused to stabilize the raw material markets, which is the only way to put an end to political and social insecurity, to offer a remedy to poverty, and to make a take-off of the economy possible.

The European effort, while significant, is thus totally inadequate to bring relief to the sufferings of two-thirds of humanity, who live on the margin of starvation (less than 2,500 calories a day) and in a perma-nent state of hunger, victims of illnesses caused by undernourish-ment and contagious diseases which strike the least resistant. Some 1,500,000,000 inhabitants of our planet have less than $100 a year at their disposal, whereas 10 per cent of the world population (all white) enjoy 80 per cent of world income. The inequality of standards of living is also striking in the field of education, and the number of illiterates is still considerable. Alongside them is a minority which monopolizes the major share of the world's riches and finds in this exploitation of men and natural resources the foundation of its pros-perity and well-being. Can anyone reasonably believe that such a situation will endure? The 'sub-proletariat' of the 'Third world' learnt to measure its strength during the struggle for emancipation; it is now aware of the inequality between Europeans and North Americans (mostly white) on the one hand, and the rest of the world on the other; will it not try one day to redress the balance? This is a serious long-term, if not medium-term, threat which Europe must work to remedy and to meet squarely.

The sufferings and carnage of an unprecedented war, the poverty and even famine that prevailed in most of Europe, coming unexpectedly after a period of precarious peace, and numerous economic and political crises – these inevitably forced people to think about the causes of the misfortunes which had been afflicting mankind for half a century, and to try to discover what remedies were possible. A system born in 1917 had claimed to furnish a solution, but this was rejected by all other governments in Europe, even though they were impressed by the Soviet Union's economic expansion and its abrupt rise to the rank of a great power. Without wishing to undertake profound structural reforms but egged on by fear of Communist contagion, the capitalist states of western Europe adopted a Welfare State system, in imitation of the New Deal and the Beveridge Plan. This was a policy of regulated economic expansion, with measures intended to ensure full employment and to banish the sufferings of the disinherited.

140, 141 The imbalance between abundance and starvation

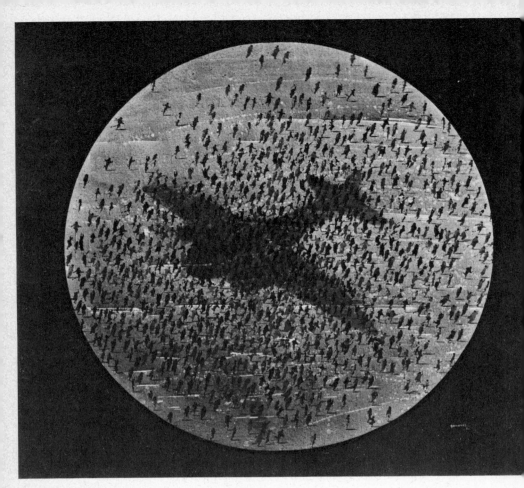

142 The shadow of atomic w
across the world; painting by
Juan Genoves (1966)

143 *Aldermaston*, painting
by Josef Herman (1962–63),
symbolizing the struggle
for atomic disarmament

But the whole period was dominated by the Cold War, in which the two greatest world powers confronted each other. It was marked by a number of international crises, by colonial wars which, though conducted with conventional weapons, were extremely deadly; and more than once there was the threat of a new world war, in which nuclear arms would inevitably have been used. Of course there were lulls, but these were quickly followed by new crises which kept up a widely diffused anxiety, a confused feeling of precariousness and uncertainty about the future, an uneasiness and disquiet whose manifestations we have seen in all spheres. 'Where', people asked, 'are we going?'

Certainly Europe has every reason to feel proud of its spectacular and astonishingly rapid recovery. Whereas it required over seventy years (1880–1953) to double the index of its industrial production, Europe achieved the same result in the following ten years (1954–63); consumption has also improved at a rate which is, perhaps, relatively small but clearly superior to anything achieved in the past. In addition, Europe still retains an important position in the world economy. Though overtaken by the United States and the USSR, and even by Japan in many areas, western Europe remains an extremely active commercial centre, the only one whose traffic extends to all parts of the globe. Eastern Europe, held back by the delay in establishing its new institutions and perhaps by an overweighted bureaucratic organization, follows the west along the same path, so that, in various degrees, the two Europes are still the centre of culture and civilization which is criticized but also envied, and which, in the long run, others would like to imitate.

Nevertheless, Europe as a whole has ceased to be the unique model which it used to be. We have seen that, alongside the great number of European technicians and experts to whom the developing nations have recourse, many others come from the USA, from China, from Israel. In the same way, the resources of Europe are not inexhaustible and the cost of exploiting them has become too high, so that its industries sometimes find it difficult to compete against other countries with a wealth of cheap labour and resources which, until recently, were still ignored or unused. One need think only of the iron mines of Lorraine and the coal-pits everywhere in Europe: the former are rivalled by the iron-ore deposits of Mauritia and Algeria, and the latter have to compete with other sources of energy such as oil, natural gas, hydroelectricity or nuclear energy, which are increasingly used. The result is that a new industrial geography, quite different from the old one, is being created before our eyes, with steelworks built 'on water', oil and gas pipelines.

It is not only from the material point of view that the former supremacy of Europe is challenged, but also in its intellectual and spiritual life. There is no doubt that it continues in very large measure to inspire writers and artists, but we have referred to the considerable influence exercised by American writers on the technique of the novel and its inspiration, as well as the influence of American artists and the wealth of American museums, to say nothing of the large number of galleries and exhibitions in the United States which has taken over Paris's role as a great art market and the arbiter of artists' reputations.

In the field of technology, Europe has – though perhaps only temporarily – lost first place. The United States' industrial supremacy is based on the very large share of the national income devoted to the education of teachers and scientists, who prepare their students for research which will further technology. In 1958 the proportion devoted to education, research, publishing and communications reached between 23 and 29 per cent of the gross national product; it rose to 40 per cent in 1968. No European country makes – or, no doubt, is in any position to make – an effort of such magnitude; only the USSR sets aside for education and research a budget of which we know little but which is surely considerable, and may even be comparable to that of the USA.

In the domain of the spirit we are witnessing a return to traditional sources in Asia and Africa. Islam is most vigorous and animated by a missionary zeal which explains its rapid progress in black Africa as compared with the Christian churches. This runs parallel with the rise of syncretic religions, most of which – even though they retain some characteristics borrowed from Christianity – are no longer really Christian. In Asia, Buddhism is having a strong renaissance, and it is well known that Christian missionaries have achieved little in India in spite of many centuries of field-work.

Above all, the very identity of Europe is threatened by the progress of industrial society which involves virtual Americanization; the survival of the European economy is conditional on the adoption of a new industrial system for which the USA supplies the most effectual example. A leading trait of the modern economy is the predominance of a few companies which produce the major part of goods and services: in the United States, for example, more than half of the total output is produced by the 500 most important corporations. They have acquired this mastery by means of their technological superiority – a superiority which requires very large capital resources, not only to pay technicians during their research, but also to construct the sophisticated machines they have invented and which may take a long time to put into operation (i.e. certain very high expenditures may not contribute to earnings for several years). This technological personnel is found not only in industrial firms, properly speaking, but also in their administrative services (such as market-research offices), in public administration and in publicity concerns. In fact, every country has need of qualified personnel, specialists in preparing indispensable plans, studying the possibilities of success in this or that market, the investment of public funds, contracts, tariffs, restrictions, etc. Thus there exists in this American industrial system, as described by J.K. Galbraith, a class of technocrats, who use computers and other electronic devices to study the information and problems submitted to them. They have considerable power and can, to a degree, dictate decisions and, in practice, usurp the authority of the elected responsible powers who, in a democratic system, are the only authentic representatives of the nation. The administrative machine has become so complex that, quite apart from its slowness, it has grown inhuman. Its exclusive preoccupations seem to be the suppression of unemployment (i.e. the most violent forms of labour discontent) and the smooth functioning of the consumers' society. The results are varied, but many are regrettable. For some it is escape: sports, travel, reading at a level which varies with the degree of the reader's education. Many seek relaxation and entertainment in detective stories and science fiction, which makes imaginative use of the contemporary cult of science and technology, and titillates the reader with extraordinary visions of an unbelievable future. Most often these create anxiety; more rarely an optimistic scientific anticipation; and occasionally a kind of religiosity. The cinema has followed in the exploitation of this vein.

More generally, the retreat of Marxism on the Left and that of ultranationalism on the Right (reborn in France for a short while during the Algerian war) have led to mistrust of any 'apocalypse', except among the Maoists and the hippies, anarchists who oppose the Communists with as much violence as they do the bourgeois. What prevails is disappointment, disillusion and bitterness against a society whose aims are devoid of ideals or grandeur, but which satisfies men's principal needs – or those, at least, which are enough for minds shaped and conditioned by radio, television and a press controlled by vested interests. That is surely the main cause of the explosion of anarchic revolt against a social organization whose standard of living – at least in the greatest part of Europe – has never before been so high, which has been so apparent, in many forms and in all social classes, for several years, especially among the young. The student revolts, which have taken place in the People's Democracies as well as in Franco's Spain, in Italy, England, West Germany and Gaullist France, certainly have many purely academic causes; but they are also characterized by material demands, and in some of them one finds a rejection of a style of living related to the American way of life, rejection of a congealed, standardized, inhuman social structure which looks on everyone only as a producer and provides no ideals, rejection of a hierarchy with fixed rules and gradations, which can only be transcended by possession of a degree or diploma not easily accessible to young people who are not born of well-to-do parents. This is the same state of mind that provokes among workers the rejection of all discipline, as demonstrated by wildcat strikes that break out without regard for pledges given and contracts made by the trade-union organizations. Even in the Church there has been opposition to the almost absolute power of the pope, to the self-satisfaction of the clergy and the state of inferiority in which, all too often, they keep the laity, whom they treat as minors and deprive of any initiative or responsibility. There is opposition on the part of the lower clergy, and opposition on the part of many laymen who demand not only effective participation in ecclesiastical administration, but also substantial independence in all areas which are not exclusively concerned with faith.

Threats of war between the great world powers, which would inevitably involve the secondary powers; social discontent in the face of the widening gulf that separates the very rich from the poor and even from people of modest means, in spite of the improvement in their standard of living; intellectual discontent among those who think that there is more to life than the acquisition of material goods (a country cottage, an automobile and gadgets that distract or lighten the burden of housewives); discouragement and disquiet among those who know in advance the more or less easy, but mediocre, life that awaits them – this is the present situation of Europe on the path of Americanization. It is true in the east as well as the west. In both halves of Europe, in spite of the obvious differences between them, it is too often the same ideal of productivity, the search for technical innovations, the increasing progress of production which are presented as the victories to be won.

From this arises a desire for liberty without check; a rejection of uniformity and of the alienation that results from the social conformities that the new industrial society intensifies; a rejection of the rule of law, and thus the negation of the conventions that constitute the social pact, without which there is nothing but violence and anarchy. These appear to be the principal tendencies of a Europe under the traumatic experience of two terrible world wars and the crimes of Nazism and Stalinism.

Nevertheless, it must be said that Europe has given evidence of an astounding power of reconstruction and an energy which implies that its creative forces are not yet exhausted. But the condition of its complete re-establishment is the disappearance of the threats we have mentioned; above all, those to peace and unity. For the world continues to be disturbed by 'little wars' which show how strong nationalism and religious intolerance still are: the war in Vietnam and in Biafra, the conflict in Northern Ireland and between Israel and the Arab states are made even worse by the arms shipments and encouragement given by the European powers and the United States to intransigent nationalist claims. In this sphere Europe has a grave responsibility, for it is using these countries as counters and perpetuating – through third parties – its old rivalries and jealousies.

We must also take account of the agitation among young people throughout the world – particularly in the universities where the future administrators of the nations are being formed. If it sometimes seems superficial, this agitation nonetheless attests to a real and deep unrest. The reaction against a large part of the heritage of the twentieth century and the rejection of all former values, which until now were contested only by utopian thinkers and professional revolutionaries, seem to have won a following which is not negligible. Even the new social and economic forms developed in the Communist world are challenged and rejected by the partisans of a libertarian revolution that tends towards anarchy. This is a proof that many institutions and traditions are no longer adapted to the industrial civilization which is progressively extending its influence over the whole globe. The formation of a great unity – the dream of Robert Schuman and Jean

Monnet – which would join Europe into one power, whose resources in raw materials, finance and labour would place it on an equal footing with the two super-powers that dominate the world, and which would undoubtedly constitute an improvement over the present situation, will not alone be enough to avert chaos and re-establish order in the human spirit. Thus profound reforms in all spheres are essential if one wants to spare Europe from declining into disorder and to protect those aspects of its heritage which deserve preservation.

144 Prisoners of industrial society; a Swiss cartoon

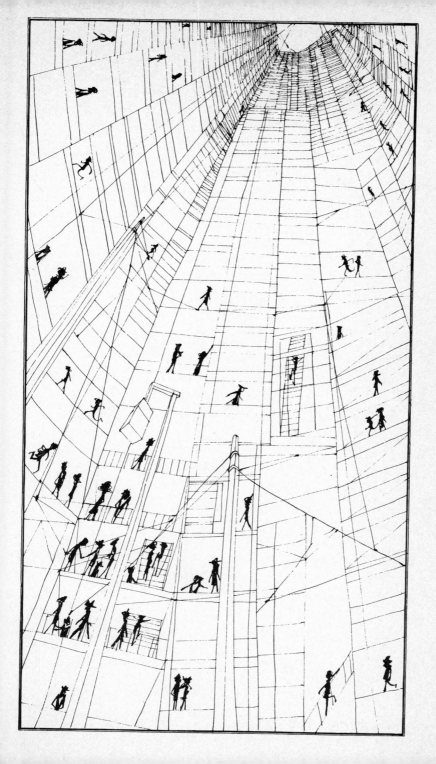

BIBLIOGRAPHICAL NOTE

The many important periodical articles which touch on our subject are not referred to here for lack of space. The works listed are those which I have found most useful in writing the book and which will help the reader who wishes to study particular topics more deeply.

GENERAL WORKS

Maurice Crouzet, *L'Epoque contemporaine* (vol. VIII of *Histoire générale des civilisations*), Paris 1968 (5th ed.), gives the broad framework of the 1914–68 period. Wolfgang Wagner, *Europa zwischen Aufbruch und Restauration. Die europäische Staatenwelt seit 1945*, Stuttgart 1968, is an excellent but purely political summary. Similar in scope are A.J. May, *Europe since 1939*, New York 1966; H. Stuart Hughes, *Contemporary Europe: a history*, New York 1966 (2nd ed.); and J. Freymond, *Western Europe since the War*, New York 1964. Peter Calvacoressi, *World Politics since 1945*, London 1968, is a succinct survey of international relations. *A New Europe?* (ed. S.R. Graubard), Boston and London 1964, contains a series of essays, some stimulating, by twenty-six contributors, on various aspects of post-war developments.

GENERAL ECONOMIC DEVELOPMENTS

For the general demographic background, see Marcel Reinhard, Jacques Dupaquier and André Armengaud, *Histoire générale de la population mondiale*, Paris 1968. More detailed are G. Frumkin, *Population Changes in Europe since 1939*, New York 1951, and J.B. Schlechtman, *Postwar Population Transfers in Europe, 1945–1955*, Philadelphia 1962. General economic histories include Shepard B. Clough and others (eds.), *Economic History of Europe: Twentieth Century*, New York 1968 (London 1969); Maurice Niveau, *Histoire des faits économiques contemporaine*, Paris 1968 (2nd ed.); and François Sellier and André Tiano, *Economie du Travail*, Paris 1967; but particularly worth reading is M.M. Postan, *An Economic History of Western Europe 1945–1964*, London 1967, and Jean de Saint-Geours, *La politique économique des principaux pays industriels de l'Occident*, Paris 1969. Jean-Jacques Servan-Schreiber, *The American Challenge*, London 1968, is a stimulating examination of United States economic penetration of Europe.

Two basic studies of the post-war development of capitalist society in the West are Andrew Shonfield, *Modern Capitalism*, London 1965, and John Kenneth Galbraith, *The Affluent Society*, New York and London 1958. Particular aspects are discussed by O. Neuloh, *Der neue Betriebsstil*, Tübingen 1960; Jean Meynaud and Dusan Sidjanski, *L'Europe des affaires. Rôle et structure des groupes*, Paris 1967; and *La mythologie des groupes financiers*, preface by Jean Meynaud, Brussels 1962; H.W. Ehrmann, *Organized Business in France*, Princeton 1957, and T. Parker (and others),

Arbeiter, Management, Mitbestimming, Stuttgart 1955, are useful on the association of workers in management; and Marcel David, *Les travailleurs et le sens de leur histoire*, Paris 1967, should be consulted on current working-class attitudes. L. Bagrit, *The Age of Automation*, London 1965, discusses the impact of automation on industry, and J. D. Bernal, *Britain's Part in the New Scientific Industrial Revolution*, London 1964, is useful in the same field.

EUROPEAN UNIFICATION
There is a vast and sometimes polemical (or ephemeral) literature on the EEC. Among more valuable works on the subject are Richard Mayne, *The Community of Europe*, New York and London 1962, and an intelligent appraisal of different tendencies by B. P. Calleo, *Europe's Future*, London 1967. Max Beloff, *The United States and the Unity of Europe*, London 1963, is valuable for the relationship of the Atlantic and European communities, and the problems arising from their conflicting interests. Other important titles are: Pierre Drouin, *L'Europe du Marché Commun*, Paris 1963; H. A. Schmitt, *The Path to European Union: from the Marshall Plan to the Common Market*, Baton Rouge 1962; E. Haas, *The Uniting of Europe*, London 1958; G. Lichtheim, *The New Europe*, New York 1964 (2nd ed.); Miriam Camps, *Britain and the European Community*, Princeton and London 1965, *European Unification in the Sixties*, New York 1966; F. Roy Willis, *France, Germany and the New Europe, 1945–1967*, Oxford 1968 (2nd ed.); K. W. Deutsch and L. J. Edinger, *France, Germany and the Western Alliance*, New York 1966. In another category, but indispensable, are Anthony Sampson, *The Anatomy of Britain*, London 1962, and *The New Europeans*, London 1968. For economic unification and its problems in eastern Europe: Istvan Agoston, *Le marché commun communiste*, Geneva 1964, and D. M. Kaser, *Comecon*, Oxford 1965.

INDIVIDUAL COUNTRIES: WESTERN EUROPE
Profitable use can be made of the works of regional geography in the *Magellan* and *Orbis* series published in Paris by Presses Universitaires de France. In the *Magellan* series, the following: Pierre George, *Panorama de monde actuel*, 1965; Pierre George and Robert Sevrin, *Belgique, Pays-Bas et Luxembourg*, 1967; Pierre Gabert and Paul Guichonnet, *Les Alpes et les Etats alpins*, 1965; Paul Chaline, *Le Royaume Uni et la République d'Irlande*, 1966; Juan Vila Valenti, *La péninsule ibérique*, 1967. In the *Orbis* series: G. Chabont, A. Guilcher and J. Beaujeu-Garnier, *L'Europe du Nord-Ouest* (3 vols); P. Birot and J. Dresch, *La Méditerranée et le Moyen-Orient* (2 vols); Pierre George and O. Tricart, *L'Europe centrale* (2 vols).

Much has been written on the transformation of French society since 1945. Among the most important studies are John Ardagh, *The New French Revolution: A Social and Economic Study of France 1945–1968*, London 1968; Gordon Wright, *The Rural Revolution in France*, Palo Alto 1969; Stanley Hoffman and others, *In Search of France*, Cambridge, Mass. 1963; as well as older books by H. Lüthy, *The State of France*, London 1955 (US edition *France Against Herself*, New York 1955); Gordon Wright, *Reshaping of French Democracy*, London 1950; D. M. Pickles, *French Politics, the first years of the Fourth Republic*, New York and London 1953, and *The Fifth French Republic*, London 1960; Philip Williams, *Politics in Post-War France*, London 1958 (2nd ed.); or the more journalistic account in Alexander Werth, *France 1940–1955*, Boston and London 1956. M. Einaudi and F. Goguel,

Christian Democracy in Italy and France, Ithaca 1952, is also important. For more specialized aspects: M. Bouvier-Ajam, *Les classes sociales en France*, Paris 1963; V. R. Lorwin, *The French Labor Movement*, Cambridge, Mass. 1954; G. Lefranc, *Le syndicalisme en France*, Paris 1968 (6th ed.); Jacques Droz, *Le socialisme démocratique, 1954–1960*, Paris 1966; J. Meynaud, *La révolte paysanne*, Paris 1963. Douglas Johnson, *France*, London 1969, is useful for general background.

For Great Britain, C. M. Woodhouse, *Post-war Britain*, London 1966, offers a good brief outline, which may be supplemented by the more impressionistic accounts of A. Marwick, *Britain in the Century of Total War*, London 1968, and Philippe Huet, *La politique économique en Grande Bretagne depuis 1945*, Paris 1969. There is valuable background information in *Social Changes in Britain*, published by the Central Office of Information, London 1962, and, for an earlier phase, A. M. Carr-Saunders and others, *A Survey of Social Conditions in England and Wales*, Oxford 1958; both of these should be read in conjunction with E. A. Johns, *The Social Structure of Modern Britain*, London 1965. R. Lewis and A. E. U. Maude have studied significant social problems in *The English Middle Classes*, London 1949, and *Professional People*, London 1952; D. Lockwood, *The Blackcoated Worker: a study in class consciousness*, London 1958, and W. L. Guttsman, *The British Political Elite*, London 1963, are also most useful. There is a considerable literature on the Welfare State, among which the works of R. M. Titmuss (*Essays of 'The Welfare State'*, London 1958; *The Irresponsible Society*, London 1960) and Richard Morris, *Income Distribution and Social Change*, London 1962, are outstanding. See also P. Goldman, *The Welfare State*, London 1964. F. Zweig, *The Worker in an Affluent Society*, London 1961, and R. Millar, *The New Classes*, London 1966, are valuable contributions to the subject; social mobility is discussed in Dr D. V. Glass (ed.), *Social Mobility in Britain*, London 1954, and F. J. Osborn and A. Whittick, *The New Towns*, London 1963, is useful on a subject also studied by C. Moindrot, *Villes et campagnes britanniques*, Paris 1967. The problems arising from the immigration of West Indians, Pakistanis and others are treated in P. Foot, *Immigration and Race in British Politics*, Harmondsworth 1966; and the following deal with new educational policies: J. Floud (and others), *Social Class and Educational Opportunity*, London 1956; J. Dulck, *L'Enseignement en Grande-Bretagne*, Paris 1968; and H. C. Dent, *Universities in Transition*, London 1961.

A short, factual introductory work on the German Federal Republic, or West Germany, now a little dated, is A. Grosser, *The Federal Republic of Germany*, New York 1964. Others include Michel Biaud, *La croissance de l'Allemagne de l'Ouest, 1949–1962*, Paris 1966; René Juilliard, *L'Europe rhénane*, Paris 1968; and – more critical in tone – H. Abosch, *L'Allemagne en mouvement*, Paris 1968. Important and illuminating, though more wide-ranging, is Ralf Dahrendorf, *Society and Democracy in Germany*, London 1968, which emphasizes changes in social structure since 1945. This is also studied in greater detail by W. Bosch, *Die Sozialstruktur in West- und Mitteldeutschland*, Bonn 1958; W. Zapf, *Wandlungen der deutschen Elite 1919–1961*, Munich 1965, and the same author's *Beiträge zur Analyse der deutschen Oberschicht*, Munich 1965 (2nd ed.). For developments in trade unions, see F. G. Dreyfus, *Le syndicalisme allemand contemporain*, Paris 1968.

In Italy, one of the main features of the post-war period is the effort to tackle the problem of the south (*Mezzogiorno*), endemic in Italian history since the foundation of the kingdom in the middle of the nineteenth century. This has been treated by J. Martarelli, *Economic Developments in Southern Italy, 1950–1960*, Washington, D.C.

1966; R. Rochefort, *Le travail en Sicile*, Paris 1961; and Giovanni Russo, *Baroni e contadini*, Bari 1955.

For Spain there is Michel Drain, *L'économie de l'Espagne*, Paris 1968; Ramón Tamames, *Introducion a la economía española*, Madrid 1969; and Juan Martinez Aliez, *La estabilidad del latifundismo*, Paris 1969. Jean Meynaud, *Les forces politiques en Grèce*, Lausanne 1968, in spite of its title, has much important economic information on Greece.

Literature on northern Europe and Scandinavia is less profuse, but W. Fleisher, *Sweden, the Welfare State*, New York 1956, and the more general accounts of Wendy Hall, *The Finns and their Country*, London 1968, and Donald S. Connery, *The Scandinavians*, London 1966, may be mentioned.

EASTERN EUROPE

Most useful in this area are Jan Marczewski, *Planification et croissance économique des democraties populaires*, 2 vols, Paris 1956; *L'Europe des pays absents*, Nancy 1958, in spite of its polemical nature; and above all the *Annuaires de l'URSS*, published since 1962 by members of the centre of research on the USSR and eastern European countries at the University of Strasbourg. Besides statistics and documents, the *Annuaires* contain fresh and solid studies of Soviet society, law, economy, international relations, as well as historical and comparative essays.

There is a general survey of recent developments in the East by S. Fischer-Galati, *Eastern Europe in the Sixties*, New York 1964. J. F. Brown, *The new Eastern Europe: the Khrushchev era and after*, London 1966, is also worth consulting. For the Soviet Union there is a useful short introduction by J. P. Nettl, *The Soviet Achievement*, London and New York 1967, but Alec Nove, *The Soviet Economy*, London 1965 (2nd ed.), is indispensable. Other general accounts include Pierre George, *L'URSS*, Paris 1962 (2nd ed.), R. W. Pethybridge, *A History of Post-War Russia*, London 1966, and Pierre Sorlin, *La société soviétique*, Paris 1967; industrial developments are discussed in W. Nutter, *Growth of Industrial Production in the Soviet Union*, Princeton 1962; and M. Miller, *Rise of the Russian Consumer*, London 1965, casts light on the changing balance of Soviet economy. R. Conquest, *Russia after Khrushchev*, London 1965, is also useful.

A general book on the People's Democracies is A. Blanc, P. George and H. Smotkine, *Les Républiques socialistes d'Europe centrale*, Paris 1967; and on Polish developments there is A. Korbonski, *Politics of Social Agriculture in Poland*, New York 1965. A. Zauberman, *Industrial Progress in Poland, Czechoslovakia and East Germany 1937–1962*, London 1964, is an important study. On East Germany, J. P. Nettl, *The Eastern Zone and Soviet Policy in Germany*, London 1951, though old, is still important; and there is a more general account by Georges Castellan, *La République démocratique allemande*, Paris 1968. A good deal of attention has been paid to Yugoslavia and the Yugoslav experiment in socialism; apart from political writings on Titoism, to which it is unnecessary to refer here, there is G. Zaninovich, *The Development of Socialist Yugoslavia*, Berkeley 1968; B. Rosier, *Agriculture moderne et socialisme. Une expérience yougoslave*, Paris 1968; and the more general works of A. W. Palmer, *Yugoslavia*, Oxford 1964, and Phyllis Auty, *Yugoslavia*, New York and London 1965.

TOWN PLANNING AND LAND DEVELOPMENT

The general works which have been found most useful are Claude Moindrot, *L'aménagement du territoire en Grande-Bretagne*, Caen 1967; Paul Clerc, *Grands ensembles et banlieues nouvelles*, Paris 1968; and Pierre Merlin, *Les « villes nouvelles »*, Paris 1969. These subjects are also discussed in 'L'Homme et la ville', *Recherches internationales*, 4th year, vols v, vii–x (1960); in two special numbers of *Architecture d'aujourd'hui* (Sept.–Nov. 1960 and Dec. 1961–Jan. 1962); and in 'Pour un bilan du siècle', a double number of *XXe siècle* (Christmas 1961).

ART AND LITERATURE

A general study of developments in French culture is Pierre de Boisdeffre, *Une histoire vivante de la littérature française d'aujourd'hui*, Paris 1968 (7th ed.). 'Le nouveau roman', in *Esprit* (July–Aug. 1958), is devoted to new trends in the writing of fiction. For the national schools of literature: Harry T. Moore, *Twentieth-Century German Literature*, New York 1967; Albert J. Farmer, *Les écrivains anglais d'aujourd'hui*, Paris 1966; Dominique Fernandez, *Le roman italien et la crise de la conscience moderne*, Paris 1958; Gianfranco Contini, *Litteratura dell'Italia unita, 1861–1968*, Florence 1968; Katherine Hunter Blair, *A Review of Soviet Literature*, London 1967. J. M. Cohen, *Poetry of this Age 1908–1958*, London 1959, is an informative study.

General surveys of the various arts are offered by Herbert Read, *A Concise History of Modern Painting*, London and New York 1959 (rev. ed. 1968), and *A Concise History of Modern Sculpture*, London and New York 1964, in addition to *Movements in Art Since 1945* by Edward Lucie-Smith, London and New York 1969, Lucy R. Lippard's *Pop Art*, London and New York 1967, *Pop Art Redefined* by John Russell and Suzi Gablik, London and New York 1969, *The New Sculpture* by Udo Kultermann, London and New York 1968.

On architecture, the following can be recommended: Bernard Champigneulle and Jean Acher, *L'architecture du XXe siècle*, Paris 1962; Michel Ragou, *Le livre de l'architecture moderne*, Paris 1958; Otto Glaus, *Highrise Building and Urban Design*, London 1967; *One-Family Housing: Solutions to an Urban Dilemma* by Hubert Hoffmann, London 1967; *Encyclopaedia of Modern Architecture*, ed. W. Pehnt, London 1963; P. Blake, *Le Corbusier. Architecture and form*, Harmondsworth 1963.

Various aspects of contemporary European life are discussed in 'Enquête sur les nationalismes', in *La Table Ronde*, March 1960; Guy Michelat and J.-P. Thomas, *Dimension du Nationalisme*, Paris 1966; Michel Amiot, *La violence dans le monde moderne*, Paris 1968; Anthony Storr, *Human Aggression*, London 1968; Julian Huxley, *The Human Crisis*, Seattle 1963; J. Ellul, *The Technological Society*, London 1965; C. P. Snow, *The Two Cultures and the Scientific Revolution*, London and New York 1959; Louis de Villefosse, *Géographie de la liberté, les droits de l'homme dans le monde*, Paris 1965; Roger Errera, *Les libertés à l'abandon*, Paris 1968; Danny Cohn-Bendit, *Obsolete Communism*, London 1968.

LIST OF ILLUSTRATIONS

1 Modern housing in the Hansa Viertel, West Berlin. Photo: Picturepoint.

2 Ossip Zadkine, *Destroyed City*, memorial monument of the May 1940 bombing of Rotterdam, 1953. Photo: Netherlands National Tourist Office.

3 The ruins of Dresden, 1945. Photo: Keystone Press Agency.

4 Leningrad in the days of the blockade. Photo: Novosti Press Agency.

5 Partisan prisoners from the series 'Gott mit uns', 1943-44, by Renato Guttuso. Photo: John R. Freeman, London.

6 *The hanged Partisan*, a bronze bas-relief in the series 'Variations on a Theme', 1939-43, by Giacomo Manzù. Collection of the artist.

7 Poster by Jerzy Karolak and Stefan Galbowski to advertise an exhibition of Polish art, 1946. Museum Narodowe, Warsaw. Photo: Bozena Seredynska, Warsaw.

8 *Europe after the Rain II*, 1940-42, painting by Max Ernst. Wadsworth Atheneum, Hartford, Connecticut, Eva Gallup Sumner and Mary Catlin Sumner Collection.

9 *Liberation*, by Ben Shahn, 1945, tempera. Collection James Thrall Soby, New Canaan, Connecticut. Photo: Museum of Modern Art, New York.

10 Russian tanks greeted as liberators at the German concentration camp at Theresienstadt (Terezin, northern Bohemia) in 1945. Drawing from the Theresienstadt diary of Jo Spiers. Jewish Historical Museum, Amsterdam.

11 *Liberation; May, 1945*, bronze relief by Henrik Starcke. Statens Museum for Kunst, Copenhagen.

12 Reconstruction in Berlin. Photo: Presse- und Informationsamt der Bundesregierung, Bonn.

13 'Warsaw – Rebuilding', 1952, poster by T. Trepkowski. Museum Narodowe, Warsaw. Photo: Bozena Seredynska, Warsaw.

14 'And yet, there will be bread', poster for the National Peasants' Party, Hungary, by G. Konecsni, 1945. Hungarian National Library, permission of the artist.

15 Renaissance and modernization of the City of London. Photo: Aerofilms.

16 A dismantled timber factory at Berlin-Neukoelln gives refuge to 30,000 East German refugees, 1953. Photo: Keystone Press Agency.

17 Comment on the German refugee problem, cartoon by M. Szewcuk, 1957.

18 *Exodus*, by Georges Rouault, 1948. Painting in a French private collection. Photo: Royal Academy of Art, London.

19 'Europe crushed by the Marshall Plan', cartoon from *Krokodil*, 1949.

20 Nationalization of the coal industry in Britain, 1947. Photo: Harold White, National Coal Board.

21 Renault assembly line. Photo: Régie Renault, Documentation Française Photothèque.

22 *Outdoor Circus*, 1948, painting by Louis Déchelette. Collection of the artist. Photo by courtesy of DuMont Schauberg, Cologne.

23 Computer advertisement, 1968-69. Honeywell Ltd, Computer Operations, Northern Europe.

24 Intensive poultry farming in Germany. Service de Presse et d'Information des Communautés Européennes. Photo: Willy François.

25 Advertisement of the British Egg Marketing Board, 1969. By courtesy of the British Egg Marketing Board.

26 'The independent peasant resists collectivization', cartoon from *Krokodil*, 1950.

27 Aerial view of car factory on the Volga. Photo: Novosti Press Agency.

28 'The strength of the rouble increased by Soviet industrial achievements', cartoon from *Krokodil*, 1949.

29 Wall newspaper showing the results of the Socialist competition to raise production of farm produce and industry in the Rostock district, East Germany, in the late 1960s. Photo: Camera Press.

30 Peat cutting by modern methods in Hungary. Photo: Interphoto MTI, Budapest.

31 The Berlin Wall from the west, and the Brandenburg Gate, behind barbed wire. Photo: Presse- und Informationsamt der Bundesregierung, Bonn.

32 East German poster, 'Economic main task', shows the West German, weighed down by a nuclear missile, losing the economic race, late 60s. Photo: Len Sirman, Camera Press.

33 Kralupy Chemical Works, Czechoslovakia, 1968. Photo: ČTK, Camera Press.

34 'Six-year plan', promotion poster by W. Gorka, 1949. Museum Narodowe, Warsaw. Photo: Bozena Seredynska.

35 Petrochemical plant in Plock, Poland, 1967. Photo: Camera Press.

36 Ironworks at Jesenice, Yugoslavia.

37 Primitive agricultural methods in Albania, 1960s. Photo: ATA, Camera Press.

38 Power station dam under construction for the Topolnitzo works in the Ihtiman District in Bulgaria, 1968. Photo: Camera Press.

39 Signing the Treaty of Rome, 25 March 1957. Photo: Service de Presse et d'Information des Communautés Européennes.

40 The Discussion, tempera and oil by Renato Guttuso, 1959–60. The Tate Gallery.

41 Paris left-wing poster, May 1968.

42 French growers jettison 40 tons of tomatoes in the river Durance, 1967. Photo: Keystone Press Agency.

43 Le Corbusier, project for St Dié.

44 Cumbernauld new town, Scotland. Photo: Aerofilms.

45 Housing development at Roehampton, London. Photo: Camera Press.

46 Munich housing development.

47 Tapiola Garden City, Finland. Photo: Pietinen, Tapiola.

48 Central precinct in Vällingby, Stockholm, 1960. Photo: Rolf Hintze.

49 Halen, near Berne. Photo: Albert Winkler, Berne.

50 Computer centre in Monteshell petrochemical factory at Brindisi. Photo: Publifoto, Milan.

51 Fully automatic piercer at work in San Cataldo potash mine, Sicily. Photo: Keystone Press Agency.

52 UNESCO building in Paris by Marcel Breuer, Pier Luigi Nervi and B.H. Zehrfuss, 1952–58. Photo: Marton, Paris. French Government Tourist Office.

53 Vickers Tower, London. Photo: J. Allan Cash.

54 Palazzo dello Sport, Rome, by Pier Luigi Nervi and Annibale Vitelozzi, 1956–57.

55 Hötorget (shopping centre), Stockholm. Photo: Mats Linden, Stockholm.

56 Metrostation Opéra, 1964, painting by Willem von Genk. Municipal Museums, Amsterdam.

57 Poster, calling for the extension of social security and early closing on Saturdays in Austria, 1961. Photo: Albertina, Vienna.

58 'Sécurité Sociale', poster by B. Villemot, 1948–49. Musée des Arts Décoratifs, Paris. Photo: Françoise Foliot.

59 Traffic jam in Place de la Concorde during nationwide strike, 21 May 1968. Photo: Keystone Press Agency.

60 Business Prospers, 1961, oil painting by Jean Dubuffet. Collection, the Museum of Modern Art, New York, Mrs Simon Guggenheim Fund.

61 'The Brain Drain', cartoon from Krokodil, 1965.

62 Advertisement for Bush Murphy colour television set, 1969. The painting featured on the screen is Cézanne's Lac d'Annecy; by courtesy of the Courtauld Institute Galleries, London.

63 The new necessities of life: Frigidaire advertisements, 1969.

64 A trans-Europe luxury express. Photo: Service de Presse et d'Information des C.E.E.

65 BOAC airline advertisement, 1969. By courtesy of BOAC.

66 Swiss rail publicity by Hans Thöni. Courtesy Graphis.

67 Russian tourists at the Tower of London, 1964. Photo: Keystone Press Agency.

68 Nordic tourists in Rome, 1965. Photo: Keystone Press Agency.

69 Helsinki City Theatre, by Timo Penttilä, 1967. Photo: Camera Press.

70 Philharmonic concert hall, West Berlin, by Hans Scharoun. Photo: Presse- und Informationsamt der Bundesregierung, Bonn.

71 Cartoon by Sempé on the contradictions of modern life, 1969.

72 Carnaby Street, London, 1968. Photo: Keystone Press Agency.

73 100,000 fans on Isle of Wight in giant marquee waiting for pop singer Bob Dylan, 1969. Photo: Keystone Press Agency.

74 Elliott boot advertisement. Dunn-Meynell, Keefe Ltd Advertising Agency. Photo: David Steward, Roy Cuthbert Studio.

75 Newly built areas of Volgograd (previously Stalingrad), 1967. Photo: Novosti Press Agency.

76 Communal television lounge in new block of flats in Moscow. Photo: Novosti Press Agency.

77 Inside Molodezhnoye cafe, Volgograd, 1967. Photo: Novosti Press Agency.

78 Soviet cartoon on inadequate transport facilities in new districts, from Krokodil, 1966.

79 Soviet cartoon showing the worker menaced by automation in capitalist countries, from *Krokodil*, 1965.

80 Street-corner sculpture from scrap-iron, by A. Jarnuszkiewicz, Elblag, Poland. Photo: Camera Press.

81 Slogans in the city centre, Stalinstadt, East Germany. Early 1960s. Photo: Dalmas, Camera Press.

82 Supermarket in Warsaw, 1965. Photo: Guy Gravett, Camera Press.

83 Belgrade's largest store in the early 1960s. Photo: Keystone Press Agency.

84 *The Chairs*, by Eugene Ionesco. Photo: Agence de Presse Bernand.

85 *Les Paravents*, by Jean Genet, Théâtre de France, Paris, 1967. Photo: Agence de Presse Bernand.

86 *Look Back in Anger*, by John Osborne, Royal Court Theatre, London, 1957. Photo: Houston Rogers.

87 *Waiting for Godot*, by Samuel Beckett, Théâtre de France, Paris, 1961. Photo: Agence de Presse Bernand.

88 *Danse Brune*, by Jean Dubuffet, 1959, Banana peel and papier maché on board. Collection Anthony Diamond, London.

89 *Composition in red and yellow* by Serge Poliakoff, 1954. Moderne Galerie Otto Stangl, Munich.

90 *Fort d'Antibes*, painting by Nicolas de Staël. Collection Jacques Dubourg, Paris.

91 *Painting*, by Maria Helena Vieira da Silva, 1953. Oil on burlap. The Solomon R. Guggenheim Museum, New York.

92 *100 F. 1957*, painting by Victor Vasarely. Galerie Denise René, Paris.

93 *T 54–16*, painting by Hans Hartung. Musée National d'Art Moderne, Paris. Photo: Jacqueline Hyde.

94 *23 mai 1953*, painting by Pierre Soulages. Collection: Tate Gallery.

95 *Still-life with Chip-Fryer*, painting by John Bratby, 1954. Collection: Tate Gallery.

96 *Just What Is It that Makes Today's Homes so Different, so Appealing?* Collage by Richard Hamilton, 1956.

97 *Piazza*, bronze by Alberto Giacometti, 1948. Collection: Peggy Guggenheim, Venice.

98 *Liegende Figur*, bronze by Fritz Wotruba. Collection: Galerie Grossleving, Düsseldorf.

99 *Grandi contatti*, bronze by Gio Pomodoro, 1962. Private collection.

100 *Enclume de rêve*, by Eduardo Chillida, 1962. Collection: Öffentliche Kunstsammlung, Basle.

101 Ballet Béjart, *Romeo et Juliette*. Photo: Agence de Presse Bernand.

102 Monica Vitti in *L'Avventura*, by M. Antonioni, Italy, 1959. Photo: National Film Archive.

103 Pierre Clementi in *Il Porcile*, by P. Pasolini, 1969. Photo: National Film Archive.

104 Delphine Seyrig in *L'Année Dernière à Marienbad*, by A. Resnais, France, 1961. Photo: National Film Archive.

105 Max von Sydow and Liv Ullman in *Skammen*, by I. Bergmann, Sweden, 1968. Photo: National Film Archive.

106 *Bicycle Thieves*, by V. de Sica, Italy, 1949.

107 Albert Finney in *Saturday Night and Sunday Morning*, by Karel Reisz, Great Britain, 1960.

108 L'unité d'habitation, Marseilles, by Le Corbusier, 1947–52.

109 Stazione Termini, Rome, built 1948–50 by Eugenio Montuori. Photo: Stato Maggiore Aeronautica Militare Italiana, Rome.

110 Pirelli head office, Milan, by Gio Ponti. Photo: Giovanni Bertolatti.

111 Phoenix-Rheinrohr headquarters building, Düsseldorf, by H. Hentrich and H. Petschnigg, 1957–60.

112 The Economist building, London, by Alison and Peter Smithson, 1961. Photo: John Donat.

113 St Catherine's College, Oxford, by A. Jacobsen, 1959–64. Photo: John Donat.

114 Sussex University, Brighton, by Sir Basil Spence. Photo: John Donat.

115 Church at Ronchamp, by Le Corbusier, 1950–54. Photo: Luvien Hervé, French Government Tourist Office.

116 Notre-Dame de Royan, by G. Gillet, 1954–59. Photo: Feuillie, French Government Tourist Office.

117 Basilica at Lourdes, by Pierre Vaga and E. Freyssinet, 1954–56. Photo: Lucien Viguin, French Government Tourist Office.

118 Coventry Cathedral, by Sir Basil Spence, 1962. Photo: J. Allan Cash.

119 Church of Marie Königin, Saarbrücken. Photo: Julius Schmidt, Saarbrücken.

120 'The Heavenly Legions', cartoon by Bo Bojeson in *Politiken*, Copenhagen, 1967. By permission of the artist.

121 Illustration advocating contraception, by Olaf Len, in *Contact*, house journal of Zanders papermakers, Germany. Permission *Graphis*, Zürich.

122 'Birth Control', poster by W. Zamecznik, Poland, 1960. Museum Narodowe, Warsaw. Photo: Bozena Seredynska.

123 'You know, I'm beginning to feel this national sport's getting really cruel . . .', cartoon by Vicky, 1963. By arrangement with the Evening Standard.

124 Cartoon by H. E. Köhler, 1957, on relationship between the franc and the Deutsche Mark, from *Der Deutsche in seiner Karikatur*, Bassermon Verlag, Stuttgart.

125 Stock Exchange, London, deserted, 15 March 1968. Photo: Keystone Press Agency.

126 Reopening of Paris Bourse after seven-day closure, November 1968. Photo: Central Press Photos.

127 Cartoon by Gibberd on the British economic crises, 1964–68. By courtesy of the *Guardian*.

128 Welsh Nationalist demonstration in Liverpool, 1965. Photo: Keystone Press Agency.

129 Nuremberg student's rally, 1961. Photo: Stefan Moses, Camera Press.

130 Insurrection in East Berlin, 1953. Photo: Camera Press.

131 Budapest battle scene, 1956. Photo: Keystone Press Agency.

132 Soviet cartoon on military government brutality in Greece, from *Krokodil*, 1968.

133 Violent repression, Paris left-wing poster, May 1968.

134 Cartoon on the police regime by Jiri Jirasek, Prague, 1968.

135 Dust jacket from Ian Fleming's book *From Russia with Love*, devised by the author, executed by R. Chopping. By courtesy of Jonathan Cape Ltd.

136 'The abduction of Europa by America', cartoon from *Krokodil*, 1966.

137 USA asking Europe to contribute to NATO costs, cartoon by Paul Flora, *Die Zeit*, 1960. By permission of the artist.

138 Japanese influence; European house interior by Eduard Ludwig at Brussels Exhibition, 1958.

139 'Last resistance to the decolonization of Africa', cartoon by Paul Flora, *Die Zeit*, 1960. By permission of the artist.

140 Ryvita advertisement for slimmers, 1969. Gallagher Smail Ltd.

141 'Help Oxfam Fight This', Oxfam fund appeal poster, 1969.

142 *The Shadow*, by Juan Genoves, 1966, oil on canvas. Marlborough Fine Art Ltd.

143 *Aldermaston*, by Josef Herman, 1962–63, oil on canvas. Artist's collection.

144 'Prisoners of the Industrial Society', drawing by Hans-Georg Rauch in *Nebelspalter*, 1970. By permission of the artist.

INDEX

References in italics denote page numbers of illustrations

Aardal aluminium plant 36
Adamov, Arthur 139
Adenauer, Konrad 61
Administrators *see* 'Third Sector'
Africa 12, 41, 63, 71, 128, 164, 166, 168, 170, 171, 175, 181, 187, 191, 192, 193, 198; *192*
Agriculture, effects of War on 9–10; post-war 29, 42–4, 49–52, 57, 59, 80, 103–8, 124, 125, 142; *43, 47, 58, 72*; Common Market policy on 62
Aillaud, Émile 158
Albania 49, 58–9, 60, 128, 129, 130, 178; *58*
Algeria 74, 93, 193, 197
Alsace-Lorraine 21
Althusser 138
Aluminium works 36, 53, 89
American Federation of Labor & Congress of Industrial Organization (AFL/CIO) 68
Amis, Kingsley 141
Anarchism 199–200
Anouilh, Jean 139
Antonioni, M. 154; *155*
Aragon, Louis 136, 139

Architecture, post-war trends 82–3, 86, 156–60; *84–5, 156–9, 161*; *see also* Housing, Town planning
Ardennes 9
Aristocracy 112–13
Asia 12, 26, 71, 170, 187, 191, 198
Athenagoras, patriarch 165
Athens Charter (1943) 75
Atomic energy 52, 62
Aubervilliers 158
Auric, Georges 152
Australia 170
Austria and Austrians 36, 63, 64, 89, 100, 108, 178; *91*
Automation 36, 38, 123; *122*
L'Avventura (Antonioni) 154; *155*

'Badajoz Plan' 82
Baierl, Helmut 139
Baku 66
Ballerup factories 160
Ballet 152; *153*
Banca d'Italia 33
Banca di Napoli 33
Banca Nazionale del Lavoro 33
Bank of England 36

Banks 31, 32–3, 35, 39, 48, 89
Bardot, Brigitte 154
Barth, Karl 165
Basso, Lelio 72
Beaudouin, Eugène 158
Beauvoir, Simone de 139
Beckett, Samuel 139; *143*
Béjart Ballet Company 152; *153*
Belgium 10, 26, 29, 34, 39–40, 41, 44, 61, 63, 75, 83, 88, 92, 96, 99, 103, 104, 105, 109, 112, 117, 135, 169, 174, 179, 190, 193
Belgrade *133*
Benelux 61
Bennett, Richard Rodney 152
Berg, Alban 152
Bergman, Ingmar 154; *155*
Berlin, East 130; Rising (1953) 177; Wall *53*; West 183; *22*; Kaiser Wilhelm Memorial Church *18*; Philharmonic Concert Hall 159; *115*
Berlin blockade (1948) 18
Bernanos, George 140
Betti, Ugo 141
Beveridge Plan 89, 90–1, 195
Biafran War 201; *195*

Bicycle Thieves (de Sica) 154; *155*
Bilkenroth, Georg 52
Birth control 165, 169, 170–1; *171*
Blum, Léon 70
Bobigny 158
Boisdeffre, Pierre de 140
Böll, Heinrich 139
Bombing, effects of in World War II 9, 29; *8*
Bonnard, Pierre 145
Boulez, Pierre 152
'Brain drain' 100, 188, 190; *101*
Brancusi, Constantin 150
Braque, Georges 145
Bratby, John *149*
Brecht, Bertolt 139
Brief Encounter (Lean) 154
Brindisi, petro-chemical plant *81*
British Broadcasting Corporation 184
British Steel Corporation 40
Buddhism 160, 198
Buffet, Bernard 146
Bulgaria 48, 49, 58–9, 126, 127, 128, 129, 178; *59*
Butor, Michel 140

Caen University 160
Caisse des Dépôts 31
Calvino, Italo 141
Camus, Albert 139
Canada 12, 170
Caro, Anthony 150
Cassa dei Depositi e Prestiti 33
Cassa per il Mezzogiorno 80
Catholic Church 162–4, 165, 169, 179; *161*
Cela, Camille José 141
Central America 12, 170
César (Baldaccini) 150
Ceylon 170
Chabrol, Claude 154
The Chairs (Ionesco) *142*
Chardin, Pierre Teilhard de 140, 163
Chemical industry 39, 40, 52, 82, 89; *54, 55, 81*
Chillida, Eduardo 150; *151*
China 26, 66, 129, 168, 170–1, 191, 193, 197
'Christ of Montfavet' movement 160
Christian Science 160
Christliche Gewerkschaftsbewegung 68
Cinema 137, 153–4, 183, 184, 199; *155*
Claudel, Paul 140
Cléo de 5 à 7 (Varda) 154
Coal industry 29, 36, 39, 40, 52, 80, 130, 197; *35*
Cold War 15, 18, 25, 138
Collectivization 49–52, 125; *47*
Co-management 87–9, 112

Comecon 52, 59, 60, 64–6, 130, 133
Commerz Bank 32
Committee for Development Aid 193
Common Market *see* European Economic Community
Commonwealth, British 63, 92
Communism, and Catholic Church 163, 165
Communist countries 14, 15, 18, 26, 27, 28, 48–59, 60, 64–6, 125–34, 144, 165, 169, 178, 186, 193, 200, 201; *see also* individual countries
Communist parties, eastern 16; western 16, 67, 70, 73–4, 138, 180
Concentration, industrial 38–40
Confédération Française de Travailleurs Chrétiens 71
Confédération Française de Travailleurs 71, 74
Confédération Générale de Cadres 71, 112
Confédération Générale du Travail 71
Congo 74, 181, 187, 192, 193
Cooperative enterprises, eastern Europe 49–50, 57, 59, 126
Cooperative marketing, western Europe 106
Coventry 9, 86; cathedral *161*
Crawley New Town 76, 86
Credit Anstalt-Bankverein 89
Crédit National 31
Cuba 66
Cumbernauld New Town 77
Czechoslovakia 21, 25, 29, 48, 49, 51, 53, 55, 65, 66, 67, 114, 125, 126, 127, 128, 130, 154, 165, 178, 186; *17, 54*

Dallapiccola, Luigi 152
Danube, River 66
David, Marcel 73
Decolonization 191–4; *192*
Delibes, Miguel 141
Democracy, retreat of 179–81
Denmark 10, 13, 41, 44, 63, 64, 75, 83, 86, 88, 93, 100, 102, 105, 106, 135, 512, 158, 160; *17, 166*
Dery, Tibor 144
Deutsche Angestelltengewerkschaft 70
Deutsche Bank 32
Deutscher Beamtenbund 70
Deutscher Gewerkschaftsbund 68, 70, 88
Disarmament 163; *166, 196*
Djilas, Milovan 132
Döblin, Alfred 138
Dolci, Danilo 141
'Dollar gap' 29
Dorival, Bernard 145
Dresden 9, 126; *8*
Dresdner Bank 32

Drouin, Pierre 64, 87
Dubcek, Alexander 126
Dubuffet, Jean *95, 146*
Duchamp, Marcel 149
Dufy, Raoul 145
Du Gard, Roger Martin 139
Düsseldorf 159; *157*

Economic disruption caused by World War II 12–13
Economic Planning Council (Sweden) 32
Edison concern, Italy 40
Education 96–100, 124, 128, 132
Egg Marketing Board (UK), advertisement *43*
Ehrenburg, Ilya 141
Eire 10, 64, 105, 190
ELAS movement, Greece 16
Electronics 36, 38
Eliade, Mircea 144
'Embourgeoisement' 109–12
Ente Nazionale Idrocarburi (ENI) 33, 82
Erhard, Dr Ludwig 33
Ernst, Max *14*
Euratom 62, 135
'Euroafrica' 63, 191
European Coal and Steel Community 61
European Development Fund 193
European Economic Community (EEC), 32, 39, 60–4, 104, 105, 133, 176, 178, 180, 190, 193
European Free Trade Association (EFTA) 63, 133
European Investment Bank 63, 193
European Organization of Space Research 135
European Payments Union 26, 61
Existentialism 139, 140
Eyck, Aldo van 159

Fabri, Diego 141
Factory design 160
Faroe Islands 178
Fascism, post-war 175
Fédération d'Educateurs Nationales (FEN) 71
FEDOM 193
Finland 60, 78, 83, 100, 158; *79, 115*
Flins 82
Fontaine-les-Grès 160
Force Ouvrière (FO) 71
Fors works 160
France 9, 10, 13, 16, 20, 24, 28, 31, 34, 35, 39, 40, 41, 42, 44, 48, 55, 61, 63, 67, 69, 70–2, 74, 75, 78, 80, 82, 83, 87, 89, 91–2, 93, 94, 96, 98, 99, 100, 103, 104–5, 106, 108, 109, 112, 113,

'Scor...
Scotla...
Scott,...
Sculp...
Sellie...
Semp...
Serva...
Servi...
Sever...
SHA...
Shah...
Sham...
Shon...
Siber...
Sica,...
Sicily...
Silesi...
Sillit...
Silva...
Skoc...
Slov...
Smit...
Soci...
Soci...
Soci...
Soci...
Soci...
Sok...
Solz...
Sou...
Sou...
19...
Sou...
Sov...
Spa...
Spa...
1...
1...
Spc...
Spr...
Sta...

Stalin, J. 18, 27
Stalinstadt *131*
Standards of living 93–6, 113, 117, 129–30, 194
Starcke, Henrik *17*
State intervention in economy 20, 30–3, 38, 42, 44, 74–82 *passim*
Steel *see* Iron, steel and tinplate
Stevenage New Town 76, 86
Stockhausen, Karlheinz 152
Stockholm 78; *79, 85*
'Stop-go' economic system 167–8
Strikes 16, 72, 74, 112
Sussex University 159; *159*
Sweden 10, 24, 29, 30, 32, 34, 40, 41, 44, 60, 63, 64, 67, 75, 78, 83, 86, 88, 92, 93, 94, 102, 105, 109, 117, 128, 135, 152, 158, 160, 164, 193; *79, 85*
Switzerland 10, 41, 44, 63, 64, 75, 93,

Unemployment 92–3
Union of Soviet Socialist Republics (USSR) 9, 12, 13, 14, 15, 21, 25, 27, 28, 29, 38, 45–6, 48, 57, 59, 60, 64–6, 75, 83, 99, 100, 104, 116, 119–24, 130, 133, 135, 136, 141–2, 149, 152, 166, 168, 169, 176, 178, 185–6, 187, 193, 195, 197, 198; *8, 47, 120–2*
'Unités d'habitation' 86, 158; *156*
United Arab Republic 66, 71, 201
United Kingdom 9, 10, 16, 20, 24, 25, 29, 31–2, 34, 36, 40–4 *passim*, 63–8 *passim*, 75–6, 83, 88–94 *passim*, 97–109 *passim*, 112, 113, 114, 118, 119, 141, 149–54 *passim*, 159, 163, 164, 165, 168, 174, 178, 185, 190, 192, 193, 200; *19, 35, 77, 84, 111, 116, 118, 155, 157–9, 161, 172, 173, 176, 195, 196*

United Nations Educational, Scientific and Cultural Organization (UNESCO) 175; *84*
United States of America 12, 13, 15, 16, 18, 26–8, 30, 38, 42, 43, 64, 66, 68, 99, 104, 123, 133, 135, 137, 154; 168, 170, 180, 187–8, 190, 191, 193, 197, 198, 199, 200; *189*
Universities 97, 99, 160; *158–9*; extension courses 100
Urbanization 76–82 *passim*, 107–8, 119, 121–3, 126, 163

Vadim, Roger 154
Valéry, Paul 139
Varda, Agnès 154
Vasarely, Victor *148*
Venard, Claude 146
Verband der deutschen Industrie 32–3
Vercors 136
Verona 162
Vienna 108, 152
Vietnam War 183, 187, 192, 201
Villon, Jacques 145
Violence, cult of 14, 181, 183; *182*
Vittorini, Elio 141
Volgograd 119; *120–1*
Volksdeutsche 21, 24
Volkswagen concern 89
Volvo works 94

Wages 94, 96
Wain, John 141
Waiting for Godot (Beckett) *143*
Wales, separatist movement 178; *176*
Warsaw *131*
Warsaw Pact 60, 175, 178
Webern, Anton 152
Weiss, Peter 139
Welfare state 89–92, 195
Werfel, Franz 138
Wesker, Arnold 141
Williamson, Malcolm 152
Wilson, Colin 141
Wismuth concern 52
Working hours 93–4
World Bank 193
Wotruba, Fritz 150; *151*
Wouki, Zao 149

Yevtushenko, Yevgeny 142
York University 159
Yugoslavia 9, 21, 25, 48, 49, 55–8, 64, 65, 100, 130–4, 144, 154, 165, 178, 193; *56, 133*

Zadkine, O. 6
Zhdanov, A. A. 141